Boeing B-47
Stratojet

OSPREY AIR COMBAT

Boeing B-47
Stratojet

Lindsay Peacock

Published in 1987 by Osprey Publishing Limited
27A Floral Street, London WC2E 9DP
Member company of the George Philip Group
© Lindsay Peacock

Sole distributors for the USA

Osceola, Wisconsin 54020, USA

British Library Cataloguing in Publication Data

Peacock, Lindsay
   Boeing B-47 Stratojet.—(Osprey air combat)
   1. United States. *Air Force*—History
   2, B-47 bomber—History
   I. Title
   358.4'2'0973   UG1242.B6

   ISBN 0-85045-763-7

Editor Dennis Baldry

Designed by Gwyn Lewis

Filmset in Great Britain by Tameside Filmsetting
Limited, Ashton-under-Lyne, Lancashire, and printed
by BAS Printers Limited, Over Wallop, Hampshire

FRONT COVER
*One of 386 B-47Es produced by Lockheed, 23363 displays
typical Stratojet markings during the later service period.
Range limitations are highlighted by the auxiliary fuel
tanks but inflight refuelling effectively bestowed global
capability on Boeing's classic bomber*
(Boeing)

TITLE PAGES
*B-47E Stratojets of the 22nd Bomb Wing at March AFB,
California in the spring of 1956, when Strategic Air
Command's manned bomber resources were approaching
their post-war peak. The B-47 was instrumental in
bringing this about, well over 1,000 examples forming the
backbone of SAC's arsenal at this time*
(USAF via Paul Bennett)

Contents

Introduction

Despite the fact that it flew for the first time when I was barely four months old and entered service shortly after my fourth birthday, it was not until the early sixties that I first encountered the Boeing B-47 Stratojet at close quarters. Between then and the spring of 1965, when 'Reflex Action' terminated in the United Kingdom, I paid many visits to the clutch of SAC bases situated in the vicinity of Oxford and Newbury. During the course of these often-weekly expeditions I naturally saw several hundred examples of the B-47, it eventually becoming one of those types that are rather taken for granted, unlike the much larger B-52, which, by virtue of being a far rarer visitor, naturally tended to hog the limelight. It was a bit like old wallpaper, I suppose—you know it is there and you often look at it but you seldom really see it, if you know what I mean.

With the benefit of hindsight—and partly influenced, I suspect, by nostalgia—I now wish that I had paid rather more attention to the Stratojet. But I suppose it was truly a classic case of familiarity breeding contempt, backed up by boredom since B-47s at the UK bases seldom seemed to do anything apart from just sit at dispersal as they performed their three-week cycles of overseas duty, their basically grey shapes sometimes being almost invisible on those often gloomy days of winter, when it becomes hard to judge precisely where the ground ends and the sky begins.

Then, at the beginning of April 1965, they all packed up and went home for the last time, the B-47 being transformed overnight from the status of a common visitor to that of a rare sight. SAC-crewed Stratojets did not, however, fade entirely from view at that time for the 55th SRW RB-47Hs continued to operate from Upper Heyford for another couple of years, whilst the 'weather birds'—the Military Air Transport Service WB-47Es—also made occasional visits, but they tended to range farther afield and were likely to appear at almost any of the US bases in Britain.

It was one of the latter that provided me with my last glimpse of the Stratojet in flight, although I didn't know that at the time. It was at Mildenhall, probably in the winter of 1968–69, and I was just leaving Mickey's Tea Bar with a few friends, having partaken of some of the excellent coffee they served there. We had literally just got outside, when, from the direction of nearby Lakenheath, the noise of a departing jet was heard. It was obviously heading more or less straight for us and, equally obviously, was in a much different weight category to the resident F-100s since it was making what could only be described as 'a bit of a racket'.

However, since it was one of those misty days—yes, they get them in East Anglia too—the cause of all the commotion was not readily apparent and I suppose it must have been about a minute or so later when a WB-47E came into view, passing more or less directly overhead at little more than 500 ft (150 m). Not surprisingly, it was soon swallowed up by the murk but the noise level remained high as it struggled to gain altitude.

Quite why that particular incident has remained so vivid is hard to say but I suspect that it probably has something to do with the fact that a Stratojet departure was always an impressive spectacle and one that would undoubtedly horrify today's anti-pollution lobby, always assuming that they could make themselves heard and weren't asphyxiated by the clouds of black smoke spewing from six J47 engines working at full bore.

Of course, the B-47 was no less impressive in many other ways, being in many people's eyes perhaps the single most significant aircraft to be conceived, developed and produced in the post-war era. A successful marriage of the largely unproven swept-wing with the still new-fangled jet engine, the B-47

7

undoubtedly put Boeing firmly on the road to pre-eminence in the commercial aviation world, many of the lessons learned being successfully applied to a host of other later designs which originated in the Seattle drawing offices.

In view of that, it is almost inconceivable that the Stratojet has not yet been the subject of a major volume but that is indeed the case. Admittedly, there have been a handful of fairly slim works examining this type but slim is most definitely the operative word and they have inevitably failed to do justice to Boeing's creation.

This oversight is, I suspect, partly due to the rapidity with which Boeing applied the lessons it learned from the Stratojet, whilst I have no doubt that the B-47's largely unspectacular history is also a factor in its neglect for it never went to war in the most widely accepted sense of the word. Indeed, it enjoyed only a relatively brief front-line career when compared with the later B-52, but this was probably as much an accident of timing as anything else for it began to reach maturity at about the same moment as the Intercontinental Ballistic Missile (ICBM) moved from the status of an unproven concept to that of an operational system.

Once the ICBM became an effective weapon, the B-47 was doomed and it is ironic to note that it was Boeing's Minuteman which largely supplanted the Stratojet as a delivery system and, in so doing, rendered it an also-ran in the strategic nuclear balance. Less glamorous Minuteman may have been, but it was far more effective and had the virtue of being much less labour intensive. All the same, there are probably many who would far rather have spent their time in a B-47 high over Kansas than in a hole in the ground somewhere under Missouri, Montana, Wyoming or the Dakotas.

In this volume, I have attempted to redress some of the years of neglect, examining such aspects as the aircraft, its handling qualities, variants and operational deployment. Nevertheless, with only 50,000 or so words at my disposal, the resulting work can hardly claim to be all-embracing although I would hope that it is sufficiently detailed to interest those who were fortunate enough to be closely associated with the type as well as the many others who were content to view it from a distance, but who, like myself, recall it with affection.

I would also hope that it may encourage others—such as those who were intimately involved with the Stratojet in one capacity or another—to share some of their experiences and recollections with us as well as bring to the attention of publishers that there are in fact many other significant types whose stories have still to be told, for the world of aviation doesn't end with the Phantom, F-16, Spitfire, Flying Fortress, Bf 109 and Tornado.

Indeed, one could say that those types represent only a beginning. . .

Lindsay Peacock
West Drayton, Middlesex
November 1986

Chapter 1
Setting the Scene

'The Strategic Air Command will be prepared to conduct long-range offensive operations in any part of the world either independently or in co-operation with land and naval forces; to conduct maximum range reconnaissance over land or sea either independently or in co-operation with land and naval forces; to provide combat units capable of intense and sustained combat operations employing the latest and most advanced weapons; to train units and personnel for the maintenance of the strategic forces in all parts of the world; to perform such special missions as the Commanding General, Army Air Force may direct.'

This was the mission of Strategic Air Command (SAC) as perceived by Carl Spaatz, Commanding General of the US Army Air Forces, and laid down in his directive of 21 March 1946 which resulted in the establishment of this new command. On paper, it all sounds so simple but, in the reality of the spring of 1946, Spaatz was only too well aware that the task which lay ahead would at times prove almost impossible and would demand a leader with very special talents.

Accordingly, he appointed General George C Kenney to lead the fledgling command—although it was not until mid-October 1946 that the latter was able to leave his position as Senior US Military Representative on the Military Staff Committee of the United Nations and actively pursue his new appointment. As a result, during the intervening period, Major General St Clair Streett, SAC's deputy commander, served as acting commanding general.

Situated on the banks of the Potomac River, just a few miles from the seat of government in Washington, Bolling Field was selected as a suitable location for SAC headquarters, major subordinate elements at the time of its inception being the 2nd Air Force at Colorado Springs and the 311th Reconnaissance Wing at MacDill Field, Florida, although the former was replaced by the 15th Air Force just ten days later,

on 31 March 1946. Subsequently, on 7 June, the 8th Air Force was reassigned from the US Army Air Forces, Pacific, to SAC, this taking up temporary residence at MacDill before moving to Fort Worth, Texas, at the beginning of November. At that time it also assumed control of about half of the fully-equipped combat units previously assigned to the 15th AF, and it duly achieved operational status on 19 November. By then, General Kenney had arrived on the scene and one of his very first actions concerned the transfer of SAC headquarters from Bolling Field to Andrews Field, Maryland, a move which was accomplished between 15–20 October, the new headquarters officially opening for business on 21 October. Thus, by the end of 1946, the higher command infrastructure had been laid down.

But as far as operational equipment and personnel resources were concerned, the situation was far less bright. At the time of its creation, SAC inherited a motley assortment of flying units, most of which were not destined to survive to the end of the year, as well as about 100,000 personnel, 22 major installations and 30 smaller bases and facilities. Unfortunately, the process of post-war demobilization was continuing on a quite massive scale and was to have a devastating impact on SAC resources, this being best illustrated by the fact that the number of personnel assigned to the new command had fallen to just over 37,000 by December 1946.

Looking at the operational forces, the picture was equally gloomy. On its formation, SAC inherited a total of 13 bomber-equipped Combat Groups, these possessing 42 Bombardment Squadrons between them. On paper, this would appear to have been a sizeable and powerful force but the reality was rather different. For a start, several of these Groups were in the final stages of demobilization, lacking equipment and personnel.

By the end of 1946 the number of Bomb Groups had declined to nine and of those only six were

actually equipped with aircraft, each having a nominal unit establishment of 30 aircraft distributed equally between three Bomb Squadrons. Even then, the number of aircraft assigned did not in fact permit each of these six Groups to be fully equipped, for in December SAC possessed just 148 examples of the Boeing B-29 Superfortress, many of which were veterans of the war in the Pacific.

Worse still was the fact that the B-29 lacked intercontinental capability, and in 1946 SAC did not possess the overseas bases to permit forward deployment of part of its forces in the event of an emergency. Efforts to redress this deficiency—most notably with the mighty Convair B-36—were in hand, but it was to be a few more years before these came to fruition. In the meantime, SAC was forced to struggle on with inadequate equipment, minimal manning levels, and a lack of financial resources.

The one 'ace in the hole', however, centered around weaponry—the USA was at that time the only nation which had the atomic bomb, the fearsome power of which had been devastatingly demonstrated at Hiroshima and Nagasaki during the final stages of World War 2. On 1 May 1946, responsibility for

Boeing's first long-range heavy bomber was the B-29 Superfortress which played a key role in the Pacific campaign during World War 2. Subsequently, it also undertook combat in the Korean War and was for several years the mainstay of Strategic Air Command. It is perhaps best remembered as being the vehicle which delivered the atomic bombs against Hiroshima and Nagasaki in August 1945
(Boeing)

using this weapon in time of war was entrusted to SAC and, more specifically, to the 509th Composite Group at Roswell Field, New Mexico, this being the only unit within the entire SAC organization which was actually capable of operating with such weapons.

Redesignated as the 509th Bomb Group during July 1946, it provided the nucleus around which SAC's ultimately massive strategic deterrent capability was eventually built. But in 1946, in common with all other SAC bomber groups, the 509th was equipped with the B-29. A small number of aircraft

Further development of the B-29 led via the XB-29D and XB-44 to the B-50, modest quantities being built for service with SAC in the immediate post-war era. The first production version was the B-50A and one of the 79 aircraft completed is seen making a very low pass at Leeds-Bradford airport in May 1953. Almost literally bristling with 0.5-in machine guns, this example was from the 43rd Bomb Wing and carried the nickname Thunderbird (Armstrong)

were despatched to Kwajalein in the Pacific during June 1946 in order to participate in 'Operation Crossroads', the first major series of post-war nuclear tests and, coincidentally, SAC's first operation with nuclear weaponry. No less than 42,000 personnel—including substantial numbers from the Army and Navy as well as many scientists—gathered in the vicinity of Bikini Atoll, these being assigned to a temporary organization known as Task Force One. This had as its primary objective the study of nuclear effects of the atomic bomb, it being intended to detonate three of these devices, although, in the event, the first two test explosions provided sufficient data to permit cancellation of the third test. Of the two bombs used in the 'Crossroads' project, one was air-delivered by B-29 whilst the other was fixed to a ship and detonated underwater.

The 2,200-strong USAAF component was collectively known as Task Group 1.5 and it was assigned the responsibility of dropping the first weapon as well as providing airborne platforms to film and obtain scientific data relating to both explosions. Delivery of the first weapon—a Nagasaki-type device—was entrusted to Major

Woodrow Swancutt of the 509th Composite Group and this was duly released from a B-29 on 1 July, the target being a collection of 73 surplus ships lying at anchor close to the atoll. The ensuing explosion resulted in five of these vessels being sunk whilst nine more suffered severe damage from blast and shock-wave effects. SAC involvement in the underwater test which took place just over three weeks later, on 25 July, was by no means so ambitious, being limited to the provision of airborne observation platforms.

A rather less spectacular and certainly much less visible event, but one which was to chart the course for the next ten years or so, occurred during October 1946 when the B-29s of the 28th Bomb Group departed from their home base at Grand Island AAF, Nebraska, and headed northward for Alaska where they were destined to spend the next six months operating in Arctic conditions on a temporary duty (TDY) basis. Noteworthy in being the first such TDY to be performed outside the boundaries of the continental USA by a fully-fledged SAC Bomb Group, this tour ended in May 1947 when the 28th returned to the heartland, taking up residence at a new home at Rapid City AAF, South Dakota.

Significant though this event was, it was eclipsed by the so-called 'Selser Flight' of November–December 1946 which is generally acknowledged as being the first occasion on which SAC bomber aircraft were used to project the USA's global capability. Conceived in response to the destruction of two USAAF C-47s over Yugoslavia, it entailed a visit to Europe by six B-29s of the 43rd Bomb Group at Davis-Monthan AAF, Arizona, although the successful nature of this mission tended to mask the fact that it had been necessary to cannibalize a number of other B-29s in order to ensure an adequate supply of spares whilst overseas.

Logistical support was provided by a couple of Douglas C-54 Skymasters from the 1st Air Transport Unit at Roswell Field, New Mexico, these accompanying the B-29s during their travels around Europe. This deployment was not without its difficulties, however, and the transatlantic crossing seems to have been a rather traumatic affair, communications breakdowns and inadequate weather data compounding the problems which would normally be faced during such a flight. Eventually, four days after leaving Arizona, the six B-29s arrived safely at Rhein-Main Air Base on the outskirts of Frankfurt, West Germany, on 17 November. After 12 days of training activities, during which time they visited several European capitals, conducted flights along the Soviet border, and surveyed a number of possible future B-29 bases, the 43rd BG aircraft flew back across the Atlantic, having in the meantime helped to convince SAC that its tactical units should be periodically deployed

Another new bomber type which entered service with SAC in the years which immediately followed World War 2 was the massive Convair B-36. Delivery of the 'aluminium overcast' began in June 1948 to the 7th Bomb Group at Carswell, Texas, and three aircraft from this unit are seen flying in 'close' formation near Fort Worth (via David Ostrowski)

overseas for intensive training under conditions closely approximating to those which would be experienced in time of war.

Thus, in the space of a few short months, SAC had established its higher command structure, had reorganized its operating units and begun to weld them into a cohesive force, had conducted operations with nuclear weapons, and had begun to deploy bomber aircraft to air bases outside of the USA. Progress was being made in many areas but the command was still having to make do with inadequate and obsolescent equipment such as the B-29, although even here the future was looking brighter, newer bombers such as the B-36 and B-50 being in prospect. Meanwhile, far away from SAC headquarters, on the other side of the continent in Seattle, Washington, the process of manufacturing two prototypes of a new and, in many ways, revolutionary bomber had begun in June 1946 amidst conditions of great secrecy.

The first full calendar year of SAC's existence was essentially one of consolidation, but significant efforts at expansion were initiated, the number of Bomb Groups rising to 16 by the end of 1947 although only 11 of these were actually equipped with aircraft. Nevertheless, bomber resources also rose quite dramatically, some 319 B-29s being assigned to the command in December, more than twice as many as had been on hand at the end of 1946.

As far as operations were concerned, regular overseas rotation of bomber echelons kicked-off in 1947 with most activity of this nature being concentrated in the Far East and principally at Yokota, Japan, which hosted a number of B-29

squadrons between May and October. Europe was by no means neglected, however, SAC elements performing training and goodwill flights to the United Kingdom, Belgium, Germany, France, Holland and Italy, while a few intrepid crews even made it as far as Saudi Arabia.

Probably the most significant event of 1947, though, was the start of the so-called 'maximum effort' missions, these taking the form of simulated attacks on major population centres in the continental USA. Los Angeles, Kansas City, and Chicago all came under 'attack' during 1947 while New York received the attentions of no less than 101 B-29s—at that time, all the airworthy aircraft that SAC could muster—during the first such mission on 16 May. Thirty more Superfortresses were unable to participate due to spares and supply shortages. Although pretty small beer compared with the 1,000-aircraft exercises of 1956, these early efforts were nevertheless impressive and were also quite valuable in that they highlighted at an early stage the need for comprehensive and reliable communications networks to exercise command and control of bomber forces whilst in flight.

Long overdue and sorely needed modernization of the bomber force finally got under way early in 1948 with the delivery of the first B-50 to the 43rd Bomb Group at Davis-Monthan AFB, Arizona, on 20 February and this was followed in late June by the first B-36 which was assigned to the 7th Bomb Group at Carswell AFB, Texas. The former type was essentially an improved B-29, featuring more powerful engines, and was thus not an intercontinental bomber in the truest sense of the term.

However, an important innovation and one which did bestow genuine global capability on the B-50 was that of in-flight refuelling. Activation of SAC's first two tanker squadrons took place in the summer of 1948, but it was not until later in the year that these began to take delivery of suitably-configured KB-29M tanker aircraft.

Initially, SAC relied on the British-developed system of in-flight refuelling which involved the use of trailing hoses and grapnels to effect transfer and which was rather cumbersome and unwieldy. Nevertheless, it did work and its value was emphatically demonstrated in early December 1948 when a B-50A of the 43rd Bomb Group successfully completed a non-stop round trip from Carswell AFB, Texas, to Hawaii, covering 9,870 miles (15,000 km) in 41 hours 40 minutes with the aid of three in-flight refuellings. Almost as impressive was a similarly-routed flight made by a 7th Bomb Group B-36A, this covering in excess of 8,000 miles (12,600 km) in 35 hours 30 minutes, remarkably without recourse to in-flight refuelling for which the B-36 was, of course, never configured.

SAC activities were by no means confined to such epochal flights and, indeed, long-haul missions became very much the norm during this period of increasing East–West tension as the Cold War began to hot up. The most obvious manifestation of this was the Soviet blockade of Berlin which began in late June 1948 and which prompted a rapid response from SAC. By coincidence, one B-29 squadron of the 301st Bomb Group was engaged on a rotational training exercise at Furstenfeldbruck in West Germany and this was joined by the other two squadrons early in

July. Two other B-29 groups—the 28th and the 307th—were subsequently deployed to bases in England during July, the former taking up temporary residence at RAF Scampton in Lincolnshire whilst the latter's aircraft were distributed between RAF Marham in Norfolk, and RAF Waddington in Lincolnshire.

As far as SAC was concerned, though, the event which had the most far-reaching impact on the Command's fortunes occurred on 19 October when Lt Gen Curtis E LeMay relieved George Kenney as Commanding General. When dealing with such a complex character as LeMay, one could, of course, fill several volumes and still fail to do the man justice. I don't propose to attempt an in-depth character assessment here but no study of SAC would be complete without some mention of this remarkable man, who, for the next nine years, was to be synonymous with SAC and who masterminded the Command's massive expansion of the early to mid-fifties.

LeMay's perpetually dour visage brings to mind another famous—or perhaps that should be infamous—name of the fifties. I refer to J Edgar Hoover, who led the Federal Bureau of Investigation (FBI) and who was generally acknowledged as being a past master of Machiavellian machinations. Whilst LeMay was almost certainly not beyond twisting a few arms to achieve his objectives, and whilst he seems to have shared Hoover's distrust and dislike of 'goddamn pinko liberals', he does at least appear to have been much less extreme than Hoover, who, in all honesty, appears to have made Attila the Hun seem like a moderate.

Recognizing that morale would be a key factor in achieving his objectives, LeMay endeavoured to improve the lot of those who served under him, one manifestation of this being the adoption of what might best be described as a 'carrot and stick' approach which was perhaps best exemplified by the so-called 'spot promotion' programme whereby personnel who demonstrated superior ability and performance were rewarded with temporary promotions. Another area of improvement concerned accommodation, LeMay being all too well aware of the debilitating effect of poor quarters on the morale of personnel who were regularly called upon to spend extended periods on overseas duty far from home and hearth.

Aerial refuelling was a particularly significant development for SAC since it allowed medium-range bombers like the B-29 to undertake intercontinental flights without too much difficulty. Much of the responsibility for proving this new technique was entrusted to the 43rd Bomb Group, one of whose B-29s is taking fuel from a KB-29P of the 43rd Air Refuelling Squadron
(via David Ostrowski)

In addition to fine tuning initiatives such as these, LeMay also kept very much up to date with regard to 'the big picture', being involved in virtually every aspect of the re-equipment programmes of the fifties, a period in which SAC discarded the old and near obsolescent World War 2 vintage machines for an entirely new fleet of purpose-built jets, a massive undertaking which witnessed the delivery of close to 3,000 bombers alone. Indeed, it was during his tenure that the B-29, B-36, and B-50 gave way to the B-47 and B-52, and he was still at the helm almost ten years later when SAC began to lay plans to move into the missile era in a big way.

In conclusion, LeMay had what is now described as charisma. Succeeding in making his presence felt across the length and breadth of SAC—from the humblest airman to his fellow generals at headquarters—LeMay inspired, bullied, and cajoled unprecedented levels of performance from those he led, in the process transforming SAC into what was arguably the most powerful military force ever seen, and it was this that was perhaps his greatest achievement. In fairness, though, like many before him, he had his fair share of luck, being fortunate in that one of the tools that was to play such an intrinsic part in the future of SAC—the Boeing B-47 Stratojet—was already well advanced when he took command.

The first couple of years of LeMay's long term of office were marked by steady, if unspectacular, growth and by the end of 1950 the number of personnel assigned to SAC had risen to just over the 85,000 mark. Operational assets were spearheaded by 14 Bomb Groups operating a mixture of B-29s, B-36s, and B-50s, these being backed up by four Reconnaissance Groups, three Fighter Groups, and about a dozen Air Refuelling Squadrons, some of which had still to be equipped with KB-29 tankers. Visits to foreign bases for rotational training duty were becoming a familiar feature of day-to-day operations but SAC had still to acquire its first overseas bases and, as is so often the case, it was to be another conflict which provided the spur to major expansion in the size of the Command. The Korean War (1950–53) opened the financial flood-gates and was to a large extent directly responsible for making available vast sums of money to modernize all elements of the US armed forces more or less overnight. Needless to say, SAC benefitted considerably. In the space of just three years it virtually doubled in size in terms of personnnel, tactical aircraft, combat wings, and operational bases.

In fairness, the Korean War cannot take all of the credit for SAC's remarkable growth. It should be recalled that this was a time of great tension between East and West, tension that manifested itself in many ways. Anti-Soviet feeling was probably at its post-war peak and there were many who, rightly or wrongly, were of the opinion that America was the last great bastion of democracy in an increasingly dangerous world. Certainly, the climate in the USA was one of thinly-veiled hostility to the 'Red Menace'

LEFT
Viewed against the picturesque backdrop of the Grand Coulee Dam, the RB-36D was employed for long-range strategic reconnaissance from 1950 until about 1955. Initial RB-36s were delivered to the 28th SRG at Rapid City, South Dakota, this being one of four reconnaissance-dedicated outfits to use the type. Later, the RB-47 became the primary reconnaissance tool
(General Dynamics)

SAC's first multi-engined jet was the North American RB-45C Tornado, just over 30 of which were operated by the 91st SRG from Barksdale AFB, Louisiana. The Tornado's career with SAC ended in December 1953 by which time the RB-47 was fast becoming available in considerable numbers
(via David Ostrowski)

and it was hardly surprising that this provided a fertile breeding ground for those 'silver-tongued devils' who perceived the 'threat' to be everywhere and who, perhaps more alarmingly, were in a position to mould public opinion.

In such circumstances were the wilder excesses of McCarthyism perpetrated, whilst the doctrine 'might is right' also found favour in the halls of Government, a sizeable portion of America's wealth being put at the disposal of the military who, after enduring years of frustrating frugality, promptly set about gorging themselves on a rich diet of new and infinitely more capable hardware. Inevitably, LeMay made sure that SAC did not go hungry, appropriations for close to 2,000 Stratojets being made during fiscal years 1951 to 1953 whilst work on the larger and considerably more costly B-52 forged ahead at a rapid rate.

All that of course lay in the future in June 1950 when the Korean War began but SAC was soon in action, B-29s of the 22nd and 92nd Bomb Groups being despatched to augment Far East Air Force bomber resources within days of the invasion. Subsequently, the 98th and 307th BGs also departed for the combat zone and during the ensuing three years of war, B-29s assigned to FEAF's Bomber Command—predominantly made up of SAC personnel on secondment—were to deliver no less than 167,100 tons of ordnance on targets which varied from troop concentrations through airfields and supply centres to heavy industry.

Little over a year after the first B-29 raids were staged out of the bomber bases in Japan and Okinawa, the B-47 began to enter service with SAC at MacDill AFB, Florida, but it was to play no part in this conflict. Indeed, it never went to war in the generally accepted sense of the term, and the closest that the pure bomber Stratojet came to conventional conflict occurred in 1964 when consideration was given to utilizing B-47s as part of the 'Arc Light' force earmarked for combat in Vietnam. In the event, the impending phase-out of the B-47 intervened, responsibility for 'Arc Light' being entrusted solely to the B-52 Stratofortress which began to fly regular combat missions in June 1965, barely eight months before the last SAC B-47E was retired to storage at Davis-Monthan AFB, Arizona.

Examples of all four types of Boeing bomber are gathered together in this company publicity picture. Taken at Seattle in the mid-1950s, the line is headed by what appears to be a VB-17. Behind that is a B-29 and beyond that, the Stratojet is represented by a Douglas-built example from the 9th Bomb Wing. There then follows a KC-97, the line ending with the first production B-52A Stratofortress. Also in evidence are the YB-52, the Model 367-80 and yet another production B-52
(Boeing via David Ostrowski)

Chapter 2
Genesis

Like many of the great advances in the field of aviation technology, what eventually appeared as the B-47 didn't come easy, the process of evolution being subjected to many false starts and blind alleys before Boeing eventually settled on the configuration which was to become such a familiar sight in the fifties and early sixties.

Even then, it is perhaps fair to say that the B-47 was as much an accident of timing as anything else for, had the war in Europe not terminated when it did, it is quite conceivable that Boeing's first venture into jet propulsion could well have taken a very different path and perhaps been consigned into the dustbin of history, along with many of the other bomber aircraft projects which appeared at about the same time. That it did not was ultimately to rebound to Boeing's enduring advantage, for the XB-47 eventually spawned a family of jet aircraft which had the most profound influence on post-war aviation in both civil and military fields.

Some—such as the B-52 Stratofortress, KC-135 Stratotanker, 707 and 747—originated from within Boeing but others—most notably the Convair 880/990 series and the Douglas DC-8—capitalized on lessons learned the hard way during the Stratojet's protracted development.

Work on what eventually emerged as the XB-47 began during the autumn of 1943, long before the end of World War 2 and at a time when Allied fortunes were still at a fairly low ebb. By then, of course, Boeing had secured for itself a position of pre-eminence as a builder of bomber aircraft, the B-17 Flying Fortress being in almost daily action in the skies above Europe whilst the B-29 Superfortress was being readied for combat in the Pacific.

With spare capacity on their drawing boards, Boeing naturally responded to an informal US Army Air Force request to industry to conceive designs based around the use of multiple jet engines. After an uncertain start, this method of propulsion was beginning to show real promise, although in the USA, as in Great Britain, the initial applications were mainly concerned with fighter-type aircraft. Increasing reliability of this still novel means of propulsion, combined with the rather greater thrust levels being achieved by the early engines, soon led to the realization that jet power could also be successfully applied to larger aircraft and, indeed, General Electric's Schenectady, New York, facility had attained ratings of 3,750 lb st (1700 kg) with its new TG-180 axial-flow turbojet.

Of potentially greater significance, however, was the fact that this engine possessed a diameter of only 38 inches—some 10 inches less than the same company's slightly more powerful centrifugal flow I-40 (later redesignated J33)—which would permit installation in reasonably-sized wing nacelles.

With numerous bomber types then well established in production and, despite the impetus of war, with only limited funding available, the USAAF had no formal requirement for such an aircraft. However, it was anxious to pursue the promise of jet power and thus allocated some of the money set aside for reconnaissance aircraft, stipulating that although optimized for high-speed photographic reconnaissance missions, the resulting designs should be readily adaptable for use in the medium bomber role. This 'belt and braces' approach did at least have the merit of permitting design work to get under way although it did not, in the event, result in any actual hardware appearing.

Like those of most of its competitors, Boeing's initial attempt at designing a jet aeroplane was perhaps most notable for its almost total lack of innovative features, although in the circumstances which prevailed it is probably fair to say that the attempt at incorporating jet engines at all was innovative enough.

Offering a marked contrast to the ballyhoo which tends to surround significant aviation events today, roll-out of the XB-47 prototype at Seattle on 12 September 1947 was a muted affair, apparently attended only by a modest number of Boeing engineers and also observed by one or two passers-by. Few of those present can have anticipated the impact that Boeing's radical design would have on aviation in years to come (via David Ostrowski)

Known in company parlance as the Boeing Model 424, it was basically a scaled-down B-29 with four of the General Electric jet engines, these being housed in pairs in 'high-speed' nacelles slung beneath the wings. Formal submission of the Model 424 to the USAAF took place in January 1944 but the ensuing programme of evaluation in Boeing's new high-speed wind tunnel test facility revealed a number of shortcomings, of which perhaps the most significant was the fact that placement of the nacelles on the wings seriously compromised wing efficiency, giving rise to unacceptable drag characteristics as well as irregularities in lift distribution. In the light of these findings, Boeing had little option but to return to the drawing board and seek alternative locations for the engines.

Whilst Boeing's designers were beavering away trying to find an effective solution, the USAAF was itself by no means idle, spending the opening months of 1944 firming up requirements for a jet-powered medium bomber which culminated in the issue during April of a proposal requesting bids from industry.

In essence, this called for an aircraft with a maximum speed of 500 mph (805 km/h), a service ceiling of 40,000 ft (12,192 m), and a tactical radius of 1,000 miles (1609 km). After several months of study, four companies responded during December 1944, Boeing being joined in competition by North American, Glenn L Martin and Convair.

Boeing's contender—the Model 432—was a singularly unprepossessing machine, featuring a straight wing and four turbojet engines buried in the upper fuselage, these being fed by massive 'elephant ear' intakes positioned high on the fuselage sides. In

RATO-augmented Stratojet departures were always a spectacular sight as the aircraft thundered skywards leaving in its wake a thick cloud of exhaust smoke. The Perspex nose fairing and lack of underwing USAF titles on the aircraft in this picture of one such takeoff almost certainly indicate that it was one of the two Stratojet prototypes
(Boeing)

RIGHT
Another view of a RATO-assisted takeoff showing the Stratojet's slender wing and Fowler-type flaps to advantage. The main gears have completed their retraction cycle and the doors are beginning to close. Once again, the subject of this picture is almost certainly one of the XB-47 prototypes
(Boeing)

By comparison with its piston-powered predecessors, the
XB-47 was aerodynamically a much cleaner design as this
inflight study of the first prototype confirms. Noteworthy
features are the podded engines, RATO-bottle ports and
the fighter-type cockpit arrangement which provided
excellent visibility
(via Robert F Dorr)

RIGHT
With the RATO ports faired over and now lacking XB-47
inscriptions, the prototype Stratojet streams its deceleration
'chute moments before touchdown. Landing was always a
critical time but this pilot seems to have judged it nicely,
being well set for a simultaneous touchdown on both main
wheel members
(via David Ostrowski)

the event, this configuration was to be rather short-lived for, in its wisdom, the USAAF elected to award design study and mock-up contracts to all four submissions in March 1945.

This decision did, however, have a sting in its tail for it stipulated that two of the contenders should utilize four jet engines whilst the other two employed six. Thus, each of the resulting designs would have only one rival, North American's XB-45 and Convair's XB-46 falling into the former category while Boeing's XB-47 and Martin's XB-48 contested the latter.

At the same time, the Northrop Aircraft Company was also awarded a contract for the highly radical YB-49, this essentially being a jet-powered derivative of the earlier XB-35 'flying wing' design and incorporating no less than eight of the new power-plants. All five aircraft had one common feature in that they all relied on variants of the J35 turbojet engine for propulsion.

Spurred on by the award of a Phase I study contract, Boeing considered numerous other configurations, subjecting some of these to extensive wind tunnel testing, but repeatedly coming up against the stumbling block that none of these straight-winged designs were able to take full advantage of the potential offered by the jet engine.

Happily, the necessary breakthrough was not long in coming and, indeed, some of the information was already in the company's hands in April 1945—which was when Boeing first learned of the theory of sweep-back as propounded by NACA's Robert T Jones earlier that same year.

Unfortunately, the absence of experimental data to prove the concept resulted in some delay and it was not until just before the German capitulation that Jones's theory was vindicated, three Boeing engineers and aerodynamicists being part of a US Army scientific advisory group which visited German aerospace centres to learn of recent developments. Amongst the great mass of material was data about swept wings and this, coupled with interviews conducted with leading German engineers, including Adolf Buseman who had first conceived the theory some ten years earlier, prompted Boeing's George Schairer to send an urgent message back to Seattle advising them to abandon the straight-wing designs forthwith in favour of sweepback.

Subsequent wind tunnel testing—much of which was conducted by Boeing in Seattle—quickly validated the theory that the drag rise could be significantly delayed by the adoption of a swept wing, with resulting marked increases in performance. Boeing's designers set to work again, arriving at the

Model 448 in September 1945. Incorporating 35 degrees of sweep at the quarter-chord point, the 448 still relied on buried engines—although there were now six of them. Four were housed on the fuselage top in more or less the same position as on the Model 432, but these were fed by a single large intake in the extreme nose section. The other two engines were both positioned in the aft fuselage, supplied with air from flush inlets along either side of the fuselage.

Despite the fact that it was aerodynamically much cleaner than the Model 432, it was still a pretty grotesque design, although aesthetic qualities probably played no part in the decision to abandon this line of development. For a start, the air inlets were almost spectacularly inefficient—particularly the flush-mounted ones on the aft fuselage—but the USAAF was also rightly concerned with safety factors, believing that the proposed engine layout seriously compromised safety, a reasonable attitude when one recalls that early jet engines were not noted for reliability, displaying a distressing tendency to catch fire, often with quite disastrous results for both crew and machine.

Secondly, the positioning of the jet efflux nozzles above the wing created numerous problems, some, as already noted, being of a safety-related nature but there were others which signally affected predicted handling and performance qualities. Boeing conducted extensive investigations into some of these aspects, going so far as to fabricate a full-size mock-up of the proposed installation and incorporating a single J33 engine. Data resulting from this investigation pinpointed a need for heat-resistant material on the upper wing surface and on the upper portion of the aft fuselage where it was intended to accommodate fuel.

As if that wasn't bad enough, the tests also revealed a potentially more serious problem, namely air viscosity. Basically, instead of being ejected directly aft into the slipstream, the superheated exhaust gases 'stuck' to the wing and fuselage surfaces for a considerable distance, thereafter impinging on the tail surfaces and causing distortion in the downwash emanating from the wing. In addition, rudder effectiveness was reduced as a result of the slightly lower air density.

Clearly, in its present guise, the Boeing submission was less than ideal and so, once again, it was back to the drawing board.

In a matter of weeks, Boeing reassessed no less than 50 alternative engine locations, eventually opting for an arrangement whereby four of the six engines were positioned in tandem pods on pylons projecting forward and well below the wing whilst the remaining two were located on the extreme wing tips, again in pods. This configuration was particularly beneficial in that it permitted adoption of a much more slender and aerodynamically efficient fuselage whilst at the same time not compromising the swept wing's inherent efficiency.

In company nomenclature, it was known as the Model 450-1-1 and it bore a striking resemblance to the aircraft which eventually made its debut at Seattle during the summer of 1947, the most notable change incorporated in the intervening period concerning repositioning of the single engine units from the wing tips to a location well inboard and beneath the wing.

Presentation of the Model 450 design to the USAAF took place during October 1945, the company being requested by that agency in the following month to prepare and deliver a formal proposal based upon the manufacture and assembly of two flyable prototype aircraft. USAAF inspection of the B-47 mock-up occurred in April 1946, the successful clearance of this hurdle being highlighted by the award to Boeing of a letter contract supplement calling for the construction of two XB-47 test specimens at a cost of approximately $8 million. Work on these two aircraft actually got under way at Boeing's Seattle facility during June 1946 and the first of the pair was subsequently rolled out barely 15 months later, on 12 September 1947.

Most of the next three months were taken up with extensive ground testing, including taxi trials at speeds of up to 90 mph (145 km/h), before the aircraft was finally cleared for flight on 14 December. In the event, bad weather then intervened, preventing the type from getting airborne on its maiden flight for almost four days.

On the morning of 17 December, the prognosis looked no better, Boeing's chief of flight test Norman D Showalter setting a 14:00 deadline after which the long-awaited first flight would again be postponed. Eventually, though, the weather relented sufficiently to permit project pilot Robert Robbins and second pilot Scott Osler to man XB-47 serial number 46-65 which duly lifted-off from the Seattle runway shortly after the deadline expired.

Although the first flight was a cautious affair, the XB-47 seems to have been eager to take to its natural element, getting airborne after a ground roll of just 4,500 ft (1372 m), a figure which must appear unbelievably short to the many SAC pilots who were later to face the ordeal of heavyweight take-offs at high ambient temperatures when it seemed like their machine just wanted to keep on rolling clear into the next state.

Cleaning up the XB-47, Robbins took the new bomber up to an altitude of 16,500 ft (5030 m) and a speed of 300 mph (483 km/h), passing over the nearby Cascade mountain range before letting down for a long and straight approach to Larson AAF where Boeing maintained its Moses Lake, Washington, test facility. After just 27 minutes in the air, the XB-47 and terra firma were safely reunited. The Stratojet was on its way but it is doubtful if Boeing or, for that matter, the newly-established US Air Force, realized what a winner they had created at the height of that euphoric moment.

Chapter 3
The Stratojet Described

As already noted in previous chapters, the Boeing design team at Seattle took some considerable time to firm up what eventually emerged as the B-47, the process of drawing board evolution culminating in an aircraft which actually bore little relationship to the team's first tentative attempts at satisfying the USAAF's rather vague requirement. However, mute testimony to the fact that Boeing eventually got it more or less right is provided by the fact that once the Model 450 was finalized, the basic design changed little during the course of production of more than 2,000 aircraft and, of course, virtually all of Boeing's subsequent offerings—as well as those of quite a few other companies—show clear evidence of their origins in the Stratojet.

When, after 15 months of being put together on the shop floor, the first XB-47 was eventually rolled out at Seattle in September 1947, it was greeted with reactions which varied from polite concern for the mental well-being of those responsible, through disinterest to blatant disbelief that Boeing could be

XB-47 6065 returns to the ramp at Seattle at the conclusion of an early test flight. The novel landing gear arrangement comprising tandem main wheels with outriggers beneath the inboard engine pods is particularly evident in this front three-quarter view. Variations in skin tone may also be discerned on the fuselage (via Michael O'Leary)

seriously contemplating proceeding with what was evidently such an ambitious and radical project.

For a company which, barely a generation before, had been turning out biplane fighters for the US Navy, the Stratojet represented a bold venture into what was essentially still unknown territory and there were probably many casual observers who inclined to the belief that the Seattle-based giant could well end up being hugely embarrassed by attempting to move too far too fast.

That they didn't says much for the expertise of those responsible, but it should also be borne in mind that, whilst the overall package was revolutionary in appearance, the XB-47 was most definitely a classic instance of the finished sum being greater than the component parts.

In producing the Stratojet, Boeing had actually exercised a degree of conservatism—the company had wisely elected to adopt features which had already been largely proven, although it is fair to say that some aspects had admittedly only been previously employed by research vehicles. Nevertheless, the Stratojet was by no means as risky a venture as its distinctive looks suggested at first glance, but there were many hurdles to be surmounted in moving from the prototype to the production stage, Boeing being by no means so sanguine as to underestimate the magnitude of the task which lay ahead.

Since the Stratojet's primary mission was perceived as being the delivery of the still relatively new atom bomb, it automatically follows that the weapons bay was arguably the most important part of the aircraft. Not surprisingly, this was located in the fuselage, occupying the space between the main undercarriage members, and it was able to accommodate 'special' nuclear weapons or, alternatively, up to 20,000 lb (9072 kg) of 'iron' bombs for use in the conventional bombing role.

Naturally, though, it was the desire to carry and deliver nuclear devices which was most influential in design of the bomb bay and at the time that the Stratojet was conceived such weapons were still exceedingly large and heavy items. Accordingly, on both XB-47s and all ten B-47As, the weapons bay occupied almost all of the space between the fore and aft undercarriage units, this being a distinctive recognition feature of these two models. Subsequent 'miniaturization' of nuclear weapons permitted redesign of the bomb bay and, as a consequence, this was much reduced in size with effect from the B-47B which was the first definitive production variant of the Stratojet.

Although the weapons bay was probably the key feature of the fuselage, the extremely thin wing of the B-47 was unsuitable for the carriage of fuel with the result that an alternative location had to be found. Inevitably, the fuselage was selected to house fuel despite the fact that it was by no means the most desirable location because of the large centre of gravity shifts which occurred as fuel was burned off by the extremely thirsty jet engines.

As far as the Stratojet was concerned, it really

Main gears tucking away, a factory fresh B-47B departs from the Boeing plant at Seattle at the start of another flight to one of Strategic Air Command's growing number of Stratojet squadrons. Serial 49-2646 lacks tail guns, but carries the 18-bottle integral RATO installation. The generous amount of flap available is also noteworthy (Boeing via Barry Wheeler)

boiled down to a question of 'Hobson's choice', since there was no alternative, sufficient tanks being situated above the weapons bay and in the aft fuselage section to contain no less than 17,000 US gal (64,143 lit) which bestowed only barely adequate range characteristics on the type. Of course, in-flight refuelling capability meant that, in effect, the B-47's range was limited primarily by crew fatigue factors and it is interesting to note that fuel capacity was actually reduced on the B-47E model even though this, like the B-47B, featured large auxiliary underwing tanks positioned roughly mid-way between the inner and outer engine pods.

The fuselage also contained the main members of the quite distinctive bicycle undercarriage, separate two-wheel units being located directly ahead of and behind the weapons bay doors, the Stratojet in fact being the first production aircraft to employ this unusual arrangement in conjunction with small outrigger wheels fitted beneath the inboard engine nacelles. An unusual aspect of the undercarriage was that it was regularly called into action as a kind of air brake, extension of the landing gear at high altitude being a key feature of certain let-down procedures. Naturally, when employing the undercarriage in this way, care was needed so as not to exceed the limiting speed of 305 knots (564 km/h) IAS.

Of itself, a quite novel approach to overcoming the problems posed by the thin wing and the position of the bomb bay, the undercarriage was in fact evaluated thoroughly by an aircraft which rejoiced in the unflattering nickname of 'Middle River Stump Jumper'. Given the designation XB-26H, this was a much modified Martin Marauder that had been fitted with bicycle gear as part of the development of Martin's own XB-48 which employed a similar arrangement and which was undoubtedly the least aesthetically pleasing of the five bomber designs to make their flying debut during the course of 1947.

As well as housing fuel, weapons and undercarriage members, the fuselage also contained crew accommodation and this again was quite unusual in that it marked a reversal of the trend towards large numbers of crew, most recent large bomber aircraft including several gunners in their complement. Despite an empty weight which approximated closely to that of the highly successful B-29 Superfortress, the Stratojet carried a crew of just three, namely pilot, co-pilot/tail gunner and bombardier/navigator, all being housed in a pressurized compartment situated directly ahead of the wing and weapons bay.

As far as the pilot and copilot were concerned, manning the B-47 was probably more akin to being in a fighter aircraft. They occupied tandem stations beneath a long blown Plexiglass canopy which offered excellent visibility, albeit at a degree of discomfort, for the Stratojet could be a particularly hot and unpleasant working environment when on the ground prior to takeoff or in the event of problems with the air conditioning system. Canopy actuation changed during the course of B-47E production, most if not all of the fiscal year 53 examples featuring

Comparison of this picture of a late production Wichita-built B-47E with those depicting the prototype reveal numerous differences in structure and finish. The revised bomb-bay door arrangement is particularly evident as is the anti-flash white undersurface paint scheme
(via Paul Bennett)

TOP LEFT
Colloquially known as the 'Middle River Stump Jumper', XB-26H 468221 was fitted with tandem main landing gear units and outrigger wheels in order to test the validity of this configuration, which was also applied to the Martin XB-48. In this picture, Stump Jumper *appears to be assessing braking efficiency and steering qualities*
(Martin via Robert F Dorr)

ABOVE
Pilot and copilot work stations on the B-47E. Crew accommodation appears to have been quite cramped to say the least as these two Boeing employees demonstrate. For some reason, the cockpit canopy has still to be fitted to this aircraft which otherwise appears to be complete
(Boeing via Philip Chinnery)

LEFT
This close-up view of the XB-26H Marauder shows the experimental single-wheel landing gear installation to advantage. External ribbing on the fuselage sides was probably intended to strengthen the structure and was also present adjacent to the rear wheel unit
(Martin via Robert F Dorr)

a clamshell-type canopy whilst all earlier Stratojets employed the aft-sliding type, but it should be noted that crew access and egress was normally effected via a door in the lower port side of the fuselage, directly aft of the radome which housed the mapping and bombing radar.

Less fortunate than his two colleagues, the bombardier/navigator was located in the fuselage proper, manning a compartment below and forward of the command pilot. Initially, the nose section terminated in a Plexiglass bomb-aiming station, although this was subsequently deleted with effect from the B-47B variant. On the RB-47E reconnaissance model, the bombardier was replaced by a photographer who occupied the same crew station and who was also responsible for navigation. Other specialized reconnaissance models—most notably the RB-47H—carried additional crew members to operate the sophisticated electronic equipment, these occupying a separate pressurized compartment in the space where the weapons bay would normally be on the pure bomber versions.

Staying on the subject of crew accommodation, it is worth mentioning that, although the XB-47s, B-47As, and B-47Es were fitted with ejection seats as standard, these were not at first installed on the B-47B although many 'Bs did later acquire them as part of a modification package which essentially updated them to B-47E configuration, modified aircraft henceforth being known as B-47B-IIs.

Two basic types of seat—manufactured by Weber and Republic—were used by the majority of B-47s, the pilot and co-pilot ejecting upwards whilst the navigator was in the less enviable position of punching out in a downward direction. Not a problem at the kinds of altitude that the Stratojet originally operated, the possibility of a hurried departure in the traffic pattern or at low altitude following the change to low-level penetration techniques frequently prompted justifiably-anxious navigators to remind the command pilot to half-roll the B-47 in the event of ejection becoming necessary. One is nevertheless inclined to wonder how many times such pleas were overlooked in the heat of an emergency but at least the B-47 navigator was better catered for than his counterparts in the British V-bombers who were denied the 'luxury' of an ejection seat.

Moving from the extreme nose to the extreme tail, the Stratojet also broke new ground in that, when compared with most other bomber aircraft then to be found in the operational inventory, it was very lightly armed. Indeed, defensive armament consisted of just a pair of tail guns and this, too, was subjected to some improvement during the production life of the aircraft.

Although it was always intended to provide armament, neither the XB-47s nor the B-47As incorporated this as standard, but a couple of examples of the latter were employed to test the A-2 and A-5 Fire Control Systems in conjunction with a brace of 0.50 calibre machine guns. The A-2 FCS was in fact adopted for the B-47B which was initially armed with two 0.50 guns, but the B-47E introduced the more sophisticated General Electric A-5 FCS and also packed a greater punch by virtue of fitment of two M-24A1 20-mm cannon, this package being subsequently retrofitted to many B-47Bs as part of the modernization efforts aimed at improving that variant's capability.

Operation of defensive armament could be accomplished either manually or automatically. In the former case, the copilot could aim and fire the guns, using a radar scope at his station to assist in gun laying, whilst in the latter mode the FCS could detect, track and position the guns on a target, all the while employing a computer to calculate ballistic equations, and at the correct moment fire the guns electrically. Gun-laying radar was positioned in a bullet fairing at the rear of the horizontal tail directly above the aft-facing turret.

Although the gun or cannon armament constituted the only overt means of defence, the Stratojet did, of course, employ alternative methods of ensuring its survival in the event of it being called upon to engage in combat. Sophisticated electronic counter-measures equipment, for instance, would have been utilized to confuse and saturate enemy defences, such equipment often being of a highly classified nature and the subject of continual updating throughout the B-47's operational career, numerous additional bumps, bulges and other protuberances appearing as it grew to maturity.

Instances of 'add-ons' which ultimately marred the original clean lines of the Stratojet are the 'Tee-Town' ECM pods which were installed on quite a few B-47Es, notably those of the 303rd and 509th Bomb Wings. Many aircraft acquired an additional fairing beneath the aft fuselage, this also forming part of the on-board ECM suite and then, of course, there were the much modified EB-47Es of the 301st and 376th Bomb Wings, each of which carried a couple of ECM operators, or 'Ravens', in a manned capsule in the weapons bay.

Another particularly interesting feature of the fuselage structure was the provision for RATO (rocket-assisted take-off) thrust augmentation, this being a welcome bonus when operating at near maximum gross weight on a hot summer's day. In its original form as applied to the XB-47, B-47A, B-47B and some early B-47E aircraft, 18 RATO units—each

capable of generating 1,000-lb (454-kg) of thrust for a fairly short period before they burned out—were buried in the fuselage directly above the rear main undercarriage member, nine bottles being positioned on each side in banks of three. Whilst this greatly enhanced field performance, it was not perhaps the most ideal method of installation for, once expended, the empty RATO units were just so much more dead weight to lug around and for an aircraft which was underpowered throughout its life any weight saving measures were always welcome.

Consequently, a revised installation was adopted with effect from the B-47E, this being doubly advantageous in that not only did it take the form of a jettisonable package but it also significantly increased the amount of thrust augmentation available. Basically, it entailed the use of a 'horse shoe' collar fitting secured snugly under the aft fuselage behind the rear main gear, this being made up of either 20 or

The slender wing, streamlined fuselage, RATO ports and tail gun armament are all clearly visible in this fine inflight study of an RB-47E initiating a tight turn to starboard during the course of a pre-acceptance test flight from Wichita, Kansas
(Boeing)

RIGHT
The extremely slim frontal aspect of the Stratojet is all too apparent in this near head-on study of a B-47A, the clean lines of the bullet-like fuselage contours being marred only by a slight bulge for the belly-mounted radar antenna and by the cockpit canopy. Also worthy of note are the widely separated pylon-mounted engines, this method of attachment being a Boeing trademark for many years to come
(Boeing via Philip Chinnery)

30 1,000-lb (454-kg) thrust RATO bottles in three rows.

RATO configuration seems to have varied according to mission requirements, aircraft carrying a heavier payload of either fuel or weapons utilizing the 30-bottle 'collar' whilst the more lightly-loaded machines had only 20. In both instances, however, the bottles were laid out in three rows, aircraft fitted with 30 having three groups of five on each side whilst those with 20 had ten bottles on each side, the front row of four being followed by two rows of three and it is interesting to note that RATO would have been mandatory for EWO-committed Stratojets operating from British bases, the runways not being long enough to permit mission-loaded aircraft to get airborne without it. Indeed, in the event of a very hot summer, even RATO augmentation would have not been sufficient to get the B-47E airborne and in such cases the 'Reflex Action' force at the base or bases concerned would have been taken off alert status. However, whether such a situation ever arose is not known.

In practice, it was usual to select ignition about ten seconds before the pre-computed lift-off point was reached. Theoretically, this gave the crew sufficient time to check that everything was working satisfactorily before finally committing themselves to flight, for once RATO was lit it was quite literally a case of 'no going back', the units continuing to burn until all of the solid or liquid fuel had been consumed. To the casual observer, any Stratojet takeoff was a pretty noisy and impressive sight as the six engines spewed out clouds of black smoke as the aircraft struggled to get airborne, but this paled into insignificance when compared with a RATO-augmented departure when the B-47 was quite literally thrust aloft in breathtaking fashion.

For the most part, this system was extremely reliable—although it did have its failings. Aircraft were destroyed as a result of fire caused either by bottles breaking loose from their restraining mounts and igniting adjacent fuel tanks, or by vapour emanating from the nearby aft main fuel vents catching alight. In both cases a fairly spectacular

This plan view of a B-47B clearly shows the positioning of national insignia and USAF titles as well as revealing the upper surface wing and fuselage walk-way markings to good advantage
(Boeing via Michael O'Leary)

blaze usually ensued but relocation of the vents eventually eliminated the latter risk although the former continued to pose a threat right up until the time that bomber versions of the Stratojet disappeared from the SAC inventory in 1965. Incidentally, those B-47Bs which were subjected to retrofit also adopted the larger jettisonable RATO pack, but it should be noted that the RB-47E model retained the original 18-bottle configuration.

Perhaps the most outstanding feature of the Stratojet was the wing. Swept-back flying surfaces were, of course, by no means new, the Curtiss-Wright XP-55 Ascender having flown as early as 1943 whilst North American's classic Sabre entered the flight test stage just ten weeks before the Stratojet's first trip aloft. But designers of large aircraft were still very conservative to say the least, conservatism which in the early stages of the design process was shared by

Boeing, whose original XB-47 proposal was based upon the use of a straight wing.

Indeed, had the war in Europe not ended when it did, it is quite conceivable that the XB-47 might well have looked very different, for the decision to adopt swept surfaces was largely prompted by the discovery of copious amounts of data in German research centres. Although this approach looked highly promising, Boeing wisely made haste slowly, fitting swept wings to a number of models and submitting them to wind tunnel testing, which soon confirmed that significant performance benefits could be gained. Even then, Boeing still had to formally request the USAAF for permission to revamp the design and it is to the service's everlasting credit that this was forthcoming, for it was almost certainly the single most important factor in the ensuing success story.

In fact, a variety of configurations were studied before Boeing elected to adopt 35 degrees of sweep back for its new bomber, this apparently being the most suitable with regard to aerodynamic and handling qualities whilst delaying the onset of drag sufficiently to bestow a measure of performance which handsomely exceeded that of most fighters of the era. Additionally, the company opted for a wing of exceedingly slender proportions which, while not compromising performance, did create problems in that it caused considerable head-scratching when it came to finding suitable locations for the undercarriage and the engines. Horizontal tail surfaces also featured 35 degrees of sweep at the leading edge and the fin was swept back 45 degrees at the leading edge, this diminishing to 35 degrees at the quarter-chord line.

As already noted, the main undercarriage members were eventually buried in the fuselage, tandemstyle, and the positioning of the powerplants was also solved in what was then a most novel fashion.

Consideration was given to burying them in the fuselage although this was ultimately dismissed as unsatisfactory by the USAAF which, naturally, was concerned with safety, early jet engines having a distressing tendency to fail, sometimes catastrophically. A counter-proposal, put forward by the military, which recommended housing the engines in wing nacelles in traditional fashion, was unacceptable to Boeing on the grounds that this would significantly impair wing efficiency and, as a direct consequence, aircraft performance.

Eventually, Boeing turned to the idea of strut-mounted pods protruding from the wing, a number of different arrangements—including one with paired units under the wing fairly close to the fuselage and single units at the wing tips—being considered

The moderately large area of the Fowler-type flaps and positioning of the novel tandem landing gears can be seen in this underside view of a B-47E on departure. Absence of SAC insignia around the nose section indicates that this aircraft was probably photographed before delivery; it also lacks the large auxiliary fuel tanks which later became a near permanent feature of SAC Stratojets
(Boeing)

before the company finalized XB-47 design, electing to go ahead with paired podded units inboard, these being slung beneath and forward of the wing, in conjunction with single units outboard, the latter fitting much more snugly under the wing just a few feet from the tip. By opting for this configuration, Boeing eliminated much of the danger posed by engine failure whilst also greatly facilitating maintenance support. However, whilst the thin wing bestowed considerable performance advantages, it brought with it its own unique problems, some of which took time to resolve.

For instance, it was extremely flexible. It was not unknown for aileron inputs to result in the wing twisting in the opposite direction, giving rise to the phenomenon of aileron reversal. The fact that the wing was optimized for high speed performance meant that at low speed, such as during the traffic pattern, it was disinclined to quit flying. Consequently, landing rolls were always long since it took time for airspeed to bleed off to a point where effective and safe braking could be accomplished. Subsequent adoption of drag and deceleration parachutes went some way towards addressing this problem but the B-47 still required an awful lot of concrete if it was to be brought safely to a halt.

Fowler-type flaps were provided to generate additional lift for take-off and landing, these being divided into two parts, namely the inboard main section and the outboard flaperon, the latter being slotted and doubling as an aileron during take-off and landing. Normally stowed in the underside of the wing, they shifted aft and downwards a considerable way, being actuated hydraulically and providing an increase in wing area of the order of five per cent.

Primary flight control surfaces—ailerons, elevators and rudder—were also hydraulically actuated, being of the non-reversible servo-type with artificial feel and manual backup, these providing more than adequate control in the normal operating envelope. However, the extremely slender wing was also quite flexible, routinely shifting as much as five feet (1.5 m) to either side of the normal position in flight. Greater deflections were not unknown, and this flexibility did cause some problems. As already noted, aileron

The fine lines of the B-47E are clearly evident in this study of a Boeing-built aircraft as it cruises serenely over the Wichita complex at the height of Stratojet production in the mid-1950s. In the distance, the nearby city of Wichita can be easily seen while detailed study of the factory area reveals just how busy Boeing was at this time, close to 100 Stratojets being dotted around on the various parking areas
(Boeing via Robert F Dorr)

In a scene enacted at no less than three manufacturing centres during the 1950s, Stratojets destined for service with Strategic Air Command are put together at Boeing's Wichita facility. Production of the definitive B-47E variant was also undertaken by Lockheed at Marietta and by Douglas at Tulsa, these three between them eventually completing the staggering total of 1,341 B-47Es (Boeing via Philip Chinnery)

reversal was one such problem, this being a common and disturbing phenomenon at speeds of the order of 425–445 knots (786–823 km/h).

At speeds in excess of 456 knots (844 km/h), however, the ailerons became ineffective and lateral control was non-existent. Boeing expended a considerable amount of energy on trying to overcome the aileron reversal problem and enhance lateral control, eventually opting for the use of spoilers and flight-testing this feature quite extensively on a development B-47. Early trials confirmed that roll control was greatly enhanced but at a cost, since the spoilers tended to induce severe buffeting, an unwelcome feature and one that took some considerable time to overcome.

Indeed, by the time a satisfactory configuration was found, Boeing had delivered well over 1,000 Stratojets to SAC and it was decided not to proceed with retrospective modification. Nevertheless, the effort expended was by no means wasted, spoilers being adopted for the roll control system of the B-52 and KC-135 as well as all members of Boeing's phenomenally successful family of commercial jet transport aircraft, this being yet another instance of

Maintaining close formation with a tanker aircraft, the pilot and copilot of an RB-47E peer upwards. Differences in the nose contours are visible while the slipway doors for the refuelling receptacle are open, indicating that contact with the tanker is imminent
(Boeing via Paul Bennett)

RIGHT
The Stratojet's large braking parachute billows behind the second B-47A as it taxies back to the ramp at the end of a test flight. On this particular aircraft the RATO ports have been faired over. It also features what appears to be an experimental tail gun turret
(USAF via Robert F Dorr)

the Stratojet paving the way for its successors.

Virtually all Stratojets utilized six turbojet engines, the only exceptions to this rule being the YB-47C which was never completed, the XB-47D which employed mixed jet/turboprop powerplants, the CL-52 flying test bed supplied to Canada for use in development of the Orenda Iroquois (for the CF-105 Arrow fighter, which was subsequently cancelled), and a standard B-47E used to test General Electric's TF34 turbofan during the early seventies.

Both XB-47s were originally fitted with the General Electric J35-GE-2 which was rated at 3,750 lb st (1701 kg) but this engine soon gave way to the rather more powerful General Electric J47-GE-3, the re-engined second prototype flying for the first time in this form in early October 1949. Rated at 5,000 lb st (2268 kg), the 'Dash Three' version of the engine was supplanted by the 5,200 lb st (2359 kg) J47-GE-11 on the B-47A and this powerplant was also fitted to the first 87 production B-47Bs, a switch then being made to the 5,800 lb st (2631 kg) J47-GE-23.

The final variant of the General Electric turbojet to be fitted to the Stratojet was the J47-GE-25 which had a dry rating of 6,000 lb st (2722 kg), a level which could be increased by means of water alcohol injection on the '25A to a maximum of 7,200 lb st (3266 kg). This version was universally fitted to the B-47E, RB-47E, RB-47H and RB-47K models but continuing weight growth—up from the 160,000 lb (72,574 kg) figure of the XB-47 to the 221,000 lb (100, 243 kg) maximum of the B-47E—quickly swallowed up all of the thrust benefit and more.

When all six engines were functioning satisfactorily and assuming that the pilot had done his sums correctly, taking into account such criteria as field elevation and temperature, there were few problems despite the fact that the amount of power available was perhaps not all that would have been desirable.

In the event of engine failure, things tended to get pretty hairy very quickly. Indeed, in instances of failure involving either outboard engine on takeoff, it has been stated that the pilot had less than two seconds to diagnose the fault and initiate the correct remedial action before asymmetric thrust prompted an uncontrollable roll in the direction of the failed engine (i.e., if the port outer failed, the aircraft would roll to port). By any yardstick, this is a pitifully small margin for error and one which goes some way towards explaining why so many Stratojets came to a fiery and spectacular end.

In addition to the podded engines, the wing was soon pressed into service as a convenient location for the carriage of additional fuel, large auxiliary external tanks—each capable of carrying approximately 11,000 lb (4989 kg) of fuel—being fitted at about the mid-span position with effect from the B-47B onwards, although in practice these seldom seem to have been carried by reconnaissance-dedicated aircraft like the RB-47E, probably as a result of that model having greater internal fuel capacity than the standard bomber derivatives.

By its very nature, the policy of nuclear deterrence pursued by the USA at the time demanded extremely reliable communications networks to eliminate the risk of inadvertent action being taken with potentially catastrophic results.

'Positive Control' was the means by which the National Command Authorities and, by definition, SAC kept a very tight rein on the forces at its disposal and this, not surprisingly, necessitated provision of

sophisticated communications equipment on each and every B-47 that would be tasked with implementing part of the Emergency War Order (EWO). I don't propose to enter into a lengthy dissertation on all the many aspects of the 'Positive Control' doctrine, it being sufficient to say that in the event of the order to launch being given, the manned bomber force would get airborne as quickly as possible, aircraft then proceeding individually to pre-determined points situated well outside enemy territory.

There, they would orbit, awaiting voice instructions to proceed to their designated targets, this being the celebrated 'go code' of which so much has been written elsewhere. Transmission of the 'go code' would be undertaken by a variety of means from a variety of sites but receipt of this command would still not irrevocably commit a bomber to combat, it being necessary for at least two members of the crew to independently satisfy themselves that it was indeed an authentic order. Only in the presence of such confirmation would they leave the 'Positive Control' point and set about arming their weapons and penetrating enemy airspace.

Production of the Stratojet at Wichita kicked-off with the B-47A model, the first example of which (91900) was rolled-out on 1 March 1950. In the event, installation of test instrumentation and a multitude of pre-flight checks and trials meant that the maiden flight of this version did not take place until 25 June (Boeing via Robert F Dorr)

In instances where the 'Positive Control' point had been reached but no 'go code' signal had been received—possibly as a result of defective radio equipment—the orbiting bomber would automatically return to base, even though this could result in an important target being neglected. Better that than face the possibility of a crew precipitating nuclear conflict by acting independently.

Accordingly, reliable airborne communications links were—and, naturally, still are—of paramount concern and this aspect was continually updated throughout the life of the B-47, SAC progressing in March 1960 from a system whereby orders to airborne aircraft had to be passed via the Airways and Air Communications Service to the 'Short Order' HF (high frequency) single sideband system which represented a great improvement in terms of both response time and reliability. Backup systems were naturally also available in the UHF and VHF bands and by the summer of 1960 SAC was fast approaching the ability to establish radio contact with all airborne aircraft within five minutes, 'Short Order' being instrumental in bringing this about.

Collins AN/ARC-58 or RCA AN/ARC-65 transceivers fitted to bomber and tanker aircraft like the B-47 and KC-97 permitted two-way communication whilst the multiplicity of links and available routings meant that signal propagation difficulties presented fewer problems than in the past. Subsequently, SAC moved into satellite communications systems in a big way but many of these advances came too late to be employed by the B-47 on a widespread basis.

Chapter 4
Stratojet Variants — New Build Aircraft

Initial testing of the pair of XB-47 prototypes quickly confirmed that the Boeing design possessed considerable promise. It was hardly surprising that the US Air Force began to give serious consideration to ordering the type into production, but the enthusiasm which greeted the XB-47's quite startling performance was tempered by a degree of caution— probably due in no small part to the very radical nature of the design. This caution prompted the USAF to proceed in what now appears to have been an uncharacteristically timid fashion, although the fact that it was still regarded as 'the new kid on the block' by many of those in authority was probably also an influential factor in their hesitation.

Consequently, the first order—placed on 3 September 1948—was modest, calling for just ten examples of a variant to be known as the B-47A, all of which were eventually earmarked for RDT&E (research, development, test and evaluation) purposes. The sum of $37 million of fiscal year 1949 funding was set aside to cover procurement of these aircraft, construction of which began more or less immediately, these being the forerunners of no less than 1,390 Stratojets that were eventually fabricated at Boeing's factory at Wichita, Kansas, although it should be noted that a small number of these were actually assembled at the two second-source production centres established at Tulsa, Oklahoma, (by Douglas) and at Marietta, Georgia, (by Lockheed) in the early fifties.

Roll-out of the first B-47A (91900) took place at Wichita on 1 March 1950, but nearly three months were to pass before this finally got airborne for its maiden flight, much of the intervening period being occupied with installation of test instrumentation and a variety of ground checks and trials.

Eventually, with all of these hurdles safely negotiated, 91900 broke ground for the first time on 25 June, by which time Air Force attitudes concerning the future of the new bomber had hardened into certainty, this transformation being underlined in emphatic fashion when 87 examples of the first true production model—the B-47B—were ordered for service with the Strategic Air Command. They would be the first true jet bombers to join SAC and would herald the ultimate demise of the piston-powered types which had served the Command well since its creation just a few years before, although it was to take almost a decade before the last of the mighty B-36s droned into obscurity.

As far as the B-47A was concerned, the ten aircraft built were mainly utilized for airframe and engine development, although some attention was also paid to defensive fire power, most notably in the area of the fire control system, an A-2 unit being installed on the seventh aircraft (91906) whilst the ninth B-47A (91908) used an A-5 FCS, both being employed in conjunction with the then-standard tail armament of a pair of 0.50-calibre machine guns. Propulsion was furnished by six 5,200 lb st (2359 kg) General Electric J47-GE-11 turbojet engines, 18,000 lb (8165 kg) of additional take-off thrust being provided by the integral solid-fuel RATO system located in the aft fuselage section.

Long bomb-bay doors—similar to those of the XB-47—were employed by the B-47A, whilst this version also retained the Plexiglass nose and rounded fin tip of the prototypes, all three of these features being subjected to some revision before the Stratojet entered quantity production as the B-47B. Bombing and navigation radar was a K-24 unit (later K-4A) whilst the 'A model was also fitted with ejection seats, a feature which, somewhat surprisingly, was omitted on the B-47B although they returned on what eventually became the definitive model of the Stratojet, the B-47E.

The B-47B could, with some justification, claim to be the first true production version of the Stratojet, a

total of 399 eventually being built between 1950 and 1953 and it was this sub-type which was first to enter the SAC inventory, when, as related elsewhere, the MacDill-based 306th Bomb Wing received its initial example on 24 October 1951.

In fact, B-47B procurement began modestly, the original contract—awarded on 9 April 1949—covering just five aircraft but the subsequent commitment to Korea and the increasingly tense 'Cold War' inevitably meant that the USAF was soon to direct a considerable amount of its financial resources towards the procurement of more long-range and medium-range bombers.

Since the B-47 was in a class of its own with regard to the latter category, it was hardly surprising that Boeing's order book began to take on a much more healthy complexion, a massive $303.6 million order for 82 more examples of the B-47B derivative being placed during the course of fiscal year 1950. Subsequently, in fiscal year 1951, the Air Force upped the ante even further, contracting for no less than 590 examples of Boeing's bomber. Of this total, 312 were produced to B-47B standard whilst the remainder consisted of 226 B-47Es and 52

The first true production Stratojet model was the B-47A, ten examples being completed for service testing before full-scale manufacture of the B-47B. The appearance of the B-47A also heralded the involvement of Boeing's Wichita factory in the Stratojet programme, the aircraft seen here, 91900, being the first of 1,390 B-47s to be produced in Kansas. Features inherited from the XB-47 prototypes included the rounded lines of the fin cap and the transparent nose section, both being deleted on the ensuing B-47B
(US Navy via Philip Chinnery)

One of ten aircraft built for follow-on research, development, test and evaluation tasks, B-47A 91900 is cleaned-up after takeoff. The outrigger wheels have already retracted, but the main gears are still in the process of disappearing into the fuselage
(via Robert F Dorr)

reconnaissance-dedicated RB-47Es.

Flying for the first time on 26 April 1951, the B-47B incorporated a number of revisions arising from experience gained with both the XB-47 and the B-47A. Some of these revisions affected the physical appearance of the aircraft to a quite marked degree and, at the time of its debut, the B-47B was instantly recognisable when compared with the earlier models of the Stratojet marque.

Gone was the rounded fin-tip of the XB-47 and B-47A, this having been superseded by a squared-off fin. The Plexiglass nose cone provided for the bombardier/navigator was also eliminated in favour of a rather more solid structure incorporating four small windows to port and two to starboard. 'Miniaturization' of nuclear weapons also permitted a reduction in the length of the bomb bay and provision was also made for the fitment of large pylon-mounted auxiliary fuel tanks between the inboard and outboard engine pods, these tanks being jettisonable once their contents had been consumed.

Although some of the earlier B-47As had been employed to evaluate fire control systems, defensive armament was by no means universally applied to all

ten aircraft and this, too, changed on the B-47B, which standardized on a pair of aft-facing 0.50-calibre machine guns. Less obvious, but no less welcome in view of continuing weight growth, was a switch to more powerful engines, although this did not in fact take effect until production of the fiscal year 1951 examples got underway. Accordingly, the first 87 B-47Bs all retained the original 5,200 lb st (2359 kg) J47-GE-11 engine as fitted to the B-47A.

Thereafter, the 5,800 lb st (2631 kg) J47-GE-23 variant of General Electric's powerplant became standard, this representing an increase in total power output of about 11.5 per cent. Unfortunately, weight growth of the order of 20 per cent more than cancelled out the benefits of extra power when operating at the heavy end of the scale. Nevertheless, performance slightly surpassed that of the B-47A, top speed rising to 536 knots (992 km/h) at 10,600 ft (3231 m).

Undoubtedly one of the most surprising omissions, and one which probably caused crew members not a little grief, was that of ejection seats, the 'bravo Stratojet lacking these when it first appeared. They were later fitted retrospectively as part of updating initiatives which brought many B-

47Bs to a standard closely approximating to that of the B-47E.

Production of the 399 B-47Bs was undertaken solely by Boeing's huge plant at Wichita, Kansas, and this facility was soon working flat out to meet the ever-increasing demand for the new bomber, which formed the backbone of Curtis E LeMay's ambitious expansion plans. As an aside, somewhat paradoxically, it was LeMay himself who played a dominant part in bringing further development of the B-47 to a halt. It is probably fair to say that his motive was excusable, though, since he was anxious not to put the forthcoming B-52 at risk due to financial considerations.

Given the highest priority for supply of materials and use of heavy industrial machinery under the so-called 'Brickbat' scheme, even Boeing's vast amount of expertise in mass production techniques could only achieve so much. It soon became apparent that demand was beginning to exceed supply. Consequently, it was decided to establish additional production centres to accelerate the flow of new-build aircraft to SAC bomber units.

Usually, Boeing's other major factory—at Seattle, Washington—would almost certainly have been selected to assist in meeting the demand. In this case, however, production capacity at Seattle was also more or less fully occupied turning out KC-97s by the score, these coincidentally being destined to join SAC. Even more importantly, though, Seattle was

gearing up to face the challenge posed by the eight-engined B-52 and was therefore quite unable to play any further part in the B-47 programme.

Accordingly, there was little option but to turn to other manufacturers. Both Lockheed and Douglas were not exactly overstretched and they were contracted to undertake full-scale production of the forthcoming B-47E model on the very day that the B-47B took to the air for the first time.

Not surprisingly, the lead-time involved in bringing these second-source centres to the status of a going concern was fairly lengthy, but the degree of urgency which prevailed is perhaps best illustrated by the fact that just under 20 months elapsed between selection and maiden flight of the first Stratojets to roll from the new production lines established in Government-owned factories at Marietta in Georgia, and Tulsa, Oklahoma.

Admittedly, the initial aircraft were in fact B-47Bs fabricated at Wichita and shipped to Douglas and Lockheed for final assembly but even then it was no mean achievement and it did, of course, greatly accelerate both the learning process and the move to autonomous production. In the event, a total of 19 B-47Bs was involved, Douglas (Tulsa) assembling ten whilst Lockheed (Marietta) was responsible for the balance, one of which was employed as an engineering pattern/mock-up and never flown. Details of the 19 aircraft concerned may be found in the table listing Stratojet production on page 186.

To return to the B-47B, subsequent modification of about 200 aircraft led to the appearance of a variant known as the B-47B-II. Entailing fitment of many of those features which were standard equipment on the B-47E, this programme started in late 1954 and eventually rendered the modified aircraft virtually indistinguishable from the later model.

Over a period of about 18 months, Boeing's Wichita factory was responsible for this updating effort which involved installation of the J47-GE-25 engine, adoption of the jettisonable 30-unit RATO gear in place of the original integral system, provision of ejection seats for all three crew members, switching to cannon armament and the newer fire control system in lieu of the machine guns previously fitted, addition of a 16-ft (4.9-m) diameter approach parachute and rearrangement of some equipment in the crew compartment. At a later date, some modified B-47B-IIs also underwent structural strengthening as part of the 'Milk Bottle' project, this permitting a modest number of these veterans to remain in the front-line inventory until the phase-out process accelerated in the early sixties.

If the B-47B helped to establish SAC as a major operator of jet bombers, the B-47E certainly enabled it to achieve clear-cut supremacy with regard to fleet size. But the influx of well over 1,000 aircraft between 1953 and 1957 must at times have threatened to seriously overwhelm the Command's apparently inexhaustible capacity for growth.

BOTTOM LEFT
As well as RDT & E functions, some B-47As were employed to explore other features planned for the production B-47B. One area of this work concerned tail gun armament, a number of different turrets being fitted to the B-47A. This is the tenth and last example of this sub-type, which was not fitted with guns
(*USAF via Robert F Dorr*)

BELOW
Quantity production of the Stratojet was inaugurated with the B-47B which began to enter service with SAC's 306th Bomb Group in October 1951. The aircraft seen here on landing lacks gun armament and has almost certainly been converted to TB-47B standard for crew training tasks
(*USAF via Robert F Dorr*)

OVERLEAF
The flight-line at Boeing's Wichita plant, packed with newly-built examples of 'the world's fastest known bomber' being prepared for delivery. When this nighttime study of B-47Bs was taken in October 1952 the production rate was building up to its eventual peak of more than one aircraft per working day. The smart new flight test hangar in the background was specially built to accommodate up to 12 B-47s
(*Boeing via Barry Wheeler*)

Under the impetus of what closely approximated to wartime urgency, the production programme was by any standard a massive undertaking in terms of human endeavour. The cost was almost frightening, each new Bomb Wing representing an investment exceeding $75 million in aircraft alone. When one recalls that, at its peak, SAC had 28 such Wings plus five more engaged solely on reconnaissance, one begins to comprehend the sheer magnitude of the Stratojet programme.

As far as the crew were concerned, one of the most welcome features of the B-47E model must have been the installation of ejector seats—if one had listened hard enough one would probably have heard a collective sigh of relief from ready rooms at SAC bases throughout the USA. This was by no means the only revision, the B-47E actually being much improved when compared with the B-47B. Some of the benefits were offset by continued weight growth which was only partially compensated for by additional power.

Basic dry thrust of the new J47-GE-25 engine was 6,000 lb (2722 kg) while the 'dash 25A version incorporated water injection which raised the thrust to 7,200 lb (3266 kg) for takeoff (a welcome plus when operating from US bases at the height of summer, or from some overseas stations where runway length was restricted). Early production B-47Es retained the integral 18-bottle RATO installation but this was soon deleted in favour of an external rack which had no less than 30 bottles, each capable of generating 1,000 lb (454 kg) of thrust for a fairly short period before burning out. In addition to producing rather more power, the new RATO

TOP LEFT
At a later stage in their service career many B-47Bs were updated to near B-47E standard and these continued to give good service until early in the 1960s. Usually referred to as B-47B-IIs, they are represented here by an aircraft from the 320th Bomb Wing at March AFB, California (Joe Bruch via Paul Bennett)

LEFT
At first glance one could be excused for assuming that this particular Stratojet is a B-47B, the fixed RATO ports and glazed areas around the nose both being features that were inherited from the initial production model. In fact, it is an early B-47E—the seventh example of this most numerous Stratojet sub-type, to be precise—and it differed significantly from its predecessor, introducing cannon armament, new gun-laying radar, revised powerplants and ejection seats as well as being rather heavier (via Robert F Dorr)

TOP LEFT
Displayed in the static park at a British air show during the late 1950s, B-47E 12404 features markings and colours that were typical of this period. Command insignia in the form of a star-spangled sash is present on the nose section but no Wing badge is carried. Note that the 'last four' of the serial number appears on the underwing fuel tank (Aviation Photo News)

LEFT
One of a handful of B-47Es employed for continuation flying duties by SAC personnel stationed in the UK, 20448 appeared in the static display at an armed forces day event at Wethersfield in the early 1960s. Assigned to the 3920th Combat Support Group at Brize Norton, it was slightly unusual in that it lacked underwing fuel tanks while it also carried the SAC badge to port in the place normally occupied by a unit badge (J M Hughes)

ABOVE
Following the adoption of anti-flash white undersurfaces, the presentation of national insignia was confined to the top of the wing, the only identification markings visible from the side being the tail number and US Air Force titles. Although absent from this B-47E, SAC insignia was usually applied to the extreme nose section (USAF via Robert F Dorr)

system had another great benefit in that it could be jettisoned when exhausted.

Increasing weight also necessitated some beefing up of the main undercarriage members and other key structural points to reduce the possibility of fatigue failure, an objective which does not appear to have been wholly successful in view of the series of crashes which occurred in 1958 and which led directly to Project Milk Bottle.

Forward fuselage configuration remained as per the B-47B on early production machines but most of the glazed areas around the nose section soon disappeared. Defensive armament was improved through the replacement of the original o.50-calibre machine guns by two 20-mm cannon and fitment of a more sophisticated fire control system developed by General Electric.

Rather surprisingly, internal fuel capacity fell slightly. The ability to refuel in flight limited the impact this might otherwise have had and the B-47E did, of course, retain the jettisonable underwing tanks introduced by the B-47B.

Flying for the first time on 30 January 1953, production of the B-47E soon gathered pace as more and more aircraft began to flow from assembly lines in three different states. Eventually, no less than 1,341 were completed, Boeing (Wichita) being responsible for just over half, having produced 691 by the time the last aircraft (53-6244) was handed over to the 40th Bomb Wing on 24 October 1956.

As far as second-source production was concerned, the flow of new Stratojets continued for a little while longer, extending into the first quarter of 1957. Deliveries from Tulsa terminated on 27 November 1956, when the 264th B-47E to be built by Douglas was accepted by the USAF, but Lockheed's 386th and last B-47E did not enter the inventory until 7 February 1957, the same month in which the B-47 equipment programme closed following re-equipment of the 100th Bomb Wing at Pease AFB, New Hampshire.

Little over a year later, the future of the Stratojet came under a cloud when a succession of crashes

Passing abeam Stone Mountain, Georgia, during the course of a pre-acceptance test flight from Marietta, B-47E 115808 was the fifth Stratojet to be produced by Lockheed, this company eventually completing some 386 aircraft of this sub-type for service with SAC. Natural metal overall finish and small 'United States Air Force' inscriptions were typical of the time while, in common with all early production B-47Es, this aircraft retains the integral 18-bottle RATO installation just ahead of the 'star-and-bar' on the fuselage side aft of the wing
(Lockheed via Robert F Dorr)

ABOVE
*Also manufactured by Lockheed at Marietta, B-47E
20372 undergoes 'Reflex Action' alert duty at one of the
British SAC bases during the early 1960s. Markings were
typical of that era, this aircraft also featuring a 20-bottle
RATO installation beneath the aft fuselage section*
(Aviation Photo News)

TOP RIGHT
*The Douglas facility at Tulsa, Oklahoma, was the third
major centre of B-47E production, 2057 being
representative of the 264 aircraft completed here in the
mid-1950s. Lacking unit and command insignia, this
aircraft does provide visible evidence of the amount of
flexing that the wing structure could safely withstand as
close study of the leading edge confirms*
(via Robert F Dorr)

RIGHT
*Production of the RB-47E model got under way at
Wichita in 1952 and the first example was eventually
rolled-out in March 1953, making a successful maiden
flight some months later, on 3 July. This is the first RB-
47E, 15258, landing at Wichita on completion of an early
test flight. Noteworthy features are the different nose
contours and the retention of the integral RATO
installation*
(Boeing via Paul Bennett)

prompted detailed examination of the fleet, this revealing extensive fatigue-related problems, the most serious of which concerned the main wing-fuselage attachment point or 'milk bottle pin'. Stress-induced corrosion had resulted in failure on a number of aircraft but studies revealed that a fix could be developed and this was duly authorized, modification of wing-fuselage attachment points pressing ahead under the code name Project Milk Bottle. In fact, modification work was rather more extensive than the foregoing would appear to indicate, forward wing longerons also being strengthened whilst doubler plates were fitted near to the wing roots, the modified aircraft henceforth being referred to as B-47E-IIs. Not surprisingly, modification didn't come cheap for well over 1,000 aircraft were affected, but it is probably fair to say that the expenditure was justified since SAC got close to eight more years of service out of some of the aircraft involved.

In addition to the pure bomber variants already examined, three sub-types were also developed specifically to fulfil various aspects of reconnaissance.

By far the most numerous of these—if not perhaps the most useful—was the RB-47E, the first example of which was rolled out at Wichita in mid-March 1953 for ground testing before finally getting airborne on its maiden flight almost three months later, on 3 July. Eventually, a grand total of 240 RB-47Es was procured between 1953 and 1955 for service with SAC's five medium Strategic Reconnaissance Wings.

Optimized for strategic photo-reconnaissance, the RB-47E shared much common ground with the standard B-47E, employing the same engines and defensive armament. However, there were a number of significant and highly visible differences. For a start, it initially retained the fixed 18-bottle RATO installation of the B-47B model while it also had a rather longer (34 inches [0.9 m] to be precise) and more streamlined nose section and some, though not all, of the specialized bombing equipment was deleted despite the fact that the RB-47E did, on paper at least, retain a secondary bombing capability.

Generally, the weapons bay was occupied by an impressive array of photographic equipment. Up to 11 cameras could be installed, although the amount varied according to mission requirements.

This company publicity picture shows the array of camera kit that was available for use by the three-man crew of the RB-47E reconnaissance variant. Although photographic reconnaissance was the primary mission of SAC's five SRWs, the presence of bombs at the end of the equipment line-up does provide confirmation that they were also expected to be proficient in the delivery of conventional and nuclear weaponry
(Boeing via Paul Bennett)

Prior to a number of B-47Es becoming available, continuation flying requirements in the UK were satisfied by a small number of redundant RB-47Es. Photographed at a British air show, 2791 was typical of the aircraft assigned to this duty, featuring dayglo areas on the nose and tail and lacking gun armament
(Military Aircraft Photographs)

RIGHT
Employed for photo mapping and weather reconnaissance, the RB-47K was a particularly rare bird, only 15 examples being completed. Originally ordered as RB-47Es, most of the surviving examples were retired in about 1963. As far as operational use is concerned, they spent their time with the 55th SRW at Forbes, one of this wing's three squadrons utilizing the K model while the other two had RB-47Hs
(Boeing via Philip Chinnery)

Trimetrogon, split-vertical, prime vertical, forward oblique and radar cameras permitted a wealth of material to be gathered during the course of a mission, responsibility for remote control operation resting with the navigator/photographer who replaced the B-47E's bombardier-navigator, other crew members being unchanged. Since it was not possible to gain access to the camera bay whilst in flight, it was necessary to pay particularly close attention to predicted weather conditions before presetting the camera apertures. This was perhaps the least satisfactory aspect of the RB-47E for if the conditions encountered were at variance with those predicted the whole mission could well prove fruitless as far as obtaining quality imagery was concerned. Possessing the ability to obtain complete photographic coverage of a swathe of land more than 2,000 miles 3219 km) long on a single mission, the RB-47E undoubtedly represented a great improvement over older piston-engined reconnaissance types such as the RB-50 and yet it began to pass from the scene fairly quickly, falling foul of changing philosophy as well as more modern means of acquiring intelligence data.

Indeed, the very first example of the Stratojet to be retired was an RB-47E, aircraft 51-5272 being committed to long term storage at Davis-Monthan AFB, Arizona, as early as 14 October 1957, less than a month before the first RB-47E-equipped unit was deactivated, this being the 91st SRW at Lockbourne AFB, Ohio. Another SRW stood down during 1958 and this model's value as a reconnaissance tool more or less ended during the summer of that year when the two surviving RB-47E Wings were reassigned to combat crew training duties in support of the expanded ground alert procedures then being implemented throughout SAC.

Unlike the RB-47E, which was perhaps a victim of changing circumstances, the RB-47H enjoyed a long and fruitful career, being one of SAC's prime intelligence-gathering tools for more than ten years. Nevertheless, the number built was modest, only 35 such aircraft being completed by Boeing's Wichita plant.

Flying for the first time in June 1955, the RB-47H adhered closely to the now familiar physical appearance of the Stratojet, but was a vastly modified machine. On first sight, the black-tipped nose was one of the more visible indications that here was a Stratojet with a difference, but one seldom got close enough to study all of the assorted bumps and bulges that had sprouted elsewhere.

Incorporating much in the way of special electronic equipment with which to accomplish its largely clandestine and occasionally extremely hazardous task, the RB-47H carried a crew of six, comprising pilot, copilot, navigator and three EWOs (electronic warfare officers) or 'Ravens' as they were more commonly known.

Pilot, copilot and navigator occupied the standard crew stations in the forward fuselage whilst the EWOs were all housed in a cramped compartment situated in what would have been the bomb bay area on a standard Stratojet bomber. Hemmed in by receivers, indicators, recorders and sundry other items of mission-related equipment, the EWOs were almost certainly the unsung heroes of the 55th SRW's operation and they definitely drew the short straw when it came to working conditions—it was clearly no place to be if one suffered from claustrophobia.

Not surprisingly, in view of the kind of work undertaken, neither SAC nor Boeing were exactly over-communicative when discussing the RB-47H and its equipment and not too much has leaked out. It certainly carried a fair amount of sensors and antennae to identify, classify, locate and monitor electronic emissions emanating from areas under surveillance, recorders being extensively used for subsequent post-mission analysis by technicians on the ground.

The final new-build model was the RB-47K, which was primarily intended to accomplish weather reconnaissance with the secondary role of photo-reconnaissance. Serving alongside the RB-47H with the 55th SRW until about 1963, only 15 were completed by Boeing at Wichita, these being amongst the last Stratojets to be built.

Originally ordered as RB-47Es, relatively little is known of their operational usage although flights were made over Alaska on a daily basis for several years, presumably to gather data pertaining to weather conditions likely to be encountered along some, if not all, of the routings that would be used by SAC bombers in the event of war.

Chapter 5
Stratojet Variants – Modified Aircraft

In addition to the seven basic prototype and production variants discussed in the previous chapter, some 20 or so other derivatives of the Stratojet are known to have existed, these being employed on such diverse tasks as crew training, weather reconnaissance, drone control, and radio relay.

Some—such as the YB-47F and the KB-47G—were one-off aircraft assigned to highly specialized research functions, whilst others—like the WB-47E and the EB-47L—were 'produced' in modest quantities for a specific operational mission to be undertaken. Regardless of the purpose for which they were developed, all of the models described in this chapter have one thing in common: they were all modifications of existing aircraft.

Since the B-47B and B-47E variants were produced in the greatest numbers, these two models provided the basis for most of the other derivatives which eventually appeared and, for ease of reference, it will probably be best to examine such variants on the basis of original sub-type, starting with the B-47B which spawned several noteworthy and distinctly interesting offshoots, these being as follows.

DB-47B/YDB-47B A considerable amount of confusion seems to surround this particular derivative, especially the number of aircraft that were completed and, perhaps more importantly, the mission they were intended to perform. Certainly, literal translation of the aircraft designation would seem to confirm that it was ostensibly intended for service as a drone carrier, a role which by even the wildest stretch of the imagination could not possibly call for the services of 74 aircraft, this figure being the generally accepted number of DB-47Bs produced.

However, it is almost certain that the DB-47B was originally conceived to carry the Bell GAM-63 Rascal air-to-surface stand-off guided missile, a weapon which entered development during the early fifties and for which SAC at one time held high hopes. Unfortunately, despite a fairly promising start, subsequent testing of the Rascal revealed that it failed to live up to expectations and it was eventually cancelled in late November 1958, SAC electing to divert funding to the Hound Dog and Quail missile systems, both of which eventually attained operational status on the B-52.

Shortly before the Rascal's demise, it was intended to equip a single squadron of the 321st Bomb Wing (445th BS) at McCoy AFB, Florida, with this weapon. In view of the fact that there are repeated allusions to no less than 74 examples of the DB-47B being converted during production, it is by no means inconceivable that SAC's original plan was to equip several squadrons with this combination.

A likely cause of further confusion is the fact that most sources refer to the DB-47B as being unarmed, but close study of some of the aircraft which lie within the generally acknowledged serial block (51-2160/2162-2234) reveals that these were in fact fitted with tail gun armament. What has almost certainly happened is that there were actually two different DB-47B configurations, the other version being a true drone control aircraft.

YRB-47B/RB-47B The first reconnaissance-dedicated version of the Stratojet to appear was the YRB-47B, no less than 91 examples of the standard B-47B bomber being modified in the early fifties to accommodate an eight-camera sensor package in a heated capsule located in the bomb bay compartment. Although more correctly known as YRB-47Bs, these aircraft are occasionally referred to as RB-47Bs and came about as an interim measure to tide SAC over until the delayed specialist RB-47E could enter service.

In the event, these aircraft led a quite nomadic life,

serving with at least four different units during 1953–55 before reverting to conventional B-47B configuration. As far as is known, they were never deployed operationally, instead being mainly employed to fulfil crew training obligations and to permit SAC to achieve an initial operational capability (IOC) rather earlier than would otherwise have been possible.

TB-47B Intended specifically to fulfil crew training tasks, the TB-47B was perhaps most readily recognizable by virtue of the removal of the tail gun armament, this installation giving way to a smooth tail fairing very similar in appearance to that of the earlier unarmed B-47A. Less obvious, but of far greater significance in view of its principal mission, the TB-47B also featured a fourth crew position for a qualified instructor pilot or navigator as required.

Assigned initially to the 3520th Flying Training Wing (later redesignated as a Combat Crew Training Wing) at McConnell AFB, Kansas, some 66 TB-47Bs were eventually produced at two centres, Douglas modifying 48 B-47Bs to this standard at Tulsa whilst the USAF's Oklahoma City Air Materiel Area at Tinker AFB weighed in with a further 18 examples.

Crew Training Air Force TB-47B 0045 nears the moment of truth as it accelerates down the Wichita runway during the early 1950s. At that time, this Kansas airfield was a scene of intense Stratojet activity, for in addition to new-build aircraft flowing from the Boeing factory the Air Force had wisely elected to site its B-47 crew training unit at Wichita, just across the airfield from the manufacturer (via Robert F Dorr)

These Stratojets bore the brunt of the crew training task for many years, being operated by Air Training Command's 3520th FTW/CCTW until 1 July 1958. On that date, a major reorganization of training elements to support the revised alert concept resulted in SAC taking over responsibility for all B-47 combat crew training. Accordingly, the 3520th was deactivated, its mission, equipment and personnel henceforth forming part of the 4347th CCTW at the same base.

WB-47B A single example of the B-47B (51-2115) was modified to WB-47B configuration, this being employed in the weather reconnaissance role by the Military Air Transport Service's Air Weather Service for several years. Assigned to the 9th Weather Reconnaissance Group from November 1957 until November 1963, it apparently ended its life as an instructional airframe, having been supplanted in service by the forerunners of an eventual total of 34 WB-47Es.

YB-47C One of the more interesting proposals conceived by Boeing's design staff during the course of the early fifties, the YB-47C was in fact a radical revision of the basic Stratojet. It would have featured a different engine arrangement incorporating four rather than six powerplants.

The chosen engine was the Allison YJ71-A-5 which was rated at 10,090 lb st (4,577 kg) and selection of this, in conjunction with other equipment changes, initially resulted in the designation YB-56 being allocated to the four-engined Stratojet. However, since the airframe was essentially the same, the designation was subsequently changed to YB-

Contrasting dramatically with the basically natural metal and white colour scheme applied at a different point in its MATS career, WB-47B 12115 was one of the most exotically marked Stratojets when this picture was taken, the largely white airframe being liberally splattered with vivid dayglo paint. What appears to be the badge of the 55th WRS is carried on the forward main landing gear door, and a distinguished unit citation ribbon can be seen on the fuselage side. Mission-related sensors were contained in the former weapons bay area and in a compartment beneath the aft fuselage section
(via Robert F Dorr)

LEFT
Assigned to the 55th Weather Reconnaissance Squadron at McClellan AFB, California, for most if not all of its operational career with the Military Air Transport Service's Air Weather Service, 12115 was unique in being the only WB-47B conversion. As such, it cleared the way for the later WB-47E variant which was 'produced' in rather greater numbers
(via Robert F Dorr)

47C and it was decided to convert the 87th B-47B (50-082) to serve as a prototype, work on modifying this eventually being abandoned before completion, following cancellation of this project.

In the planning stage, however, a reconnaissance variant to be known as the RB-56A and, later, the RB-47C was mooted, designed to carry specialized photographic and electronic reconnaissance equipment in the space normally occupied by the weapons bay. It, too, was abandoned, as was a pure bomber model known as the B-47C.

XB-47D Although never a candidate for operational deployment, the XB-47D was rather more fortunate than the YB-47C and did enjoy a fairly lengthy career as a flying test-bed. Tasked with evaluating turbo-prop powerplants, it presented a most bizarre appearance. It utilized mixed jet/turboprop pro-pulsion, the inboard pairs of podded J47s giving way to single examples of the 9,710-eshp Wright YT49-W-1 whilst the outboard J47s were retained.

Two aircraft—51-2046 and 51-2103—were mod-ified to XB-47D configuration, both employing 15-ft (4.6-m) diameter propellers featuring massive 'paddle'-type blades bestowing a performance which approximated closely to that of the standard Stratojet. Normal empty weight was 79,800 lb (36,196 kg) whilst gross take-off weight was more than double that at 184,428 lb (83,655 kg) and the XB-47D eventually attained a maximum speed of 597 mph (961 km/h) at 13,500 ft (4,115 m). Service ceiling was some 33,750 ft (10,287 m) with rate of climb at normal power being of the order of 2,900 ft (884 m) per minute. Modification work was accomplished during the course of 1955 and the XB-47D duly got airborne for its maiden flight on 26 August of that year, 51-2103 being the first of the pair to fly.

YB-47F Although SAC introduced the Boeing-developed 'flying boom' system of aerial refuelling in the autumn of 1950 when the first example of the KB-29P was delivered, the Command appears to have been by no means certain that this was the most suitable method for wide-scale adoption and testing of alternatives continued for some time afterwards, evidence of this being provided by the YB-47F/KB-47G project which evaluated the probe-and-drogue method of fuel transfer during the course of 1952.

Two modified Stratojets were involved in these

RIGHT
With 'two turning and two burning', and with the sun just beginning to disperse early morning mist at Seattle, the second XB-47D (12103) taxies to the end of the runway at the start of another test flight. Both of the XB-47D test vehicles were based on standard production B-47B airframes and were capable of performance which closely approximated to that of the B-47B
(via Robert F Dorr)

BELOW
Although best known as a pure jet, Boeing's medium bomber also served as a test-bed for other methods of propulsion. Most startling from the viewpoint of appearance was the XB-47D, which utilized mixed turbine/turbojet powerplants in the mid-1950s. Two aircraft were eventually modified to this configuration to test the Curtiss-Wright T49 turboprop, employing one of these engines in place of each inner pair of podded jets. Driving massive 15-ft diameter 'paddles', the XB-47D also featured modified flap assemblies and revised instruments and controls
(Boeing)

trials, the single YB-47F (50-009) acting as the receiver aircraft and being fitted with an in-flight refuelling probe in the extreme nose section directly ahead of the cockpit. Although apparently successful, SAC elected to go for the Boeing system in a big way and, by 1952, the Command had begun to take delivery of large numbers of the boom-equipped Boeing KC-97 Stratofreighter, this item of equipment ultimately being adopted as standard for all SAC tankers.

Accordingly, following this evaluation, the probe-and-drogue method was abandoned, at least as far as SAC was concerned, although it was used extensively by Tactical Air Command for a number of years.

KB-47G The other element of the in-flight refuelling test programme accomplished in 1952 was the KB-47G, a single B-47B (50-040) being configured to serve as the tanker aircraft. In this instance, however, the necessary modification work was rather more extensive and entailed fitment of a hose and drogue assembly in the weapons bay, this being employed successfully on a number of occasions and demonstrating that the KB-47G would have made a good tanker. In addition to that portion of the evaluation programme accomplished in concert with the YB-47F, the KB-47G also transferred fuel to a Republic F-84G Thunderjet before the project was abandoned.

CL-52 Another engine test-bed, this rather unusual designation was in fact a Canadair model number and was applied to a B-47B (51-2059) that was supplied to the Royal Canadian Air Force on a loan basis during

Two more one-off examples of the Stratojet family were the YB-47F and KB-47G. The front aircraft (0040) is the KB-47G, which was the world's first jet-powered tanker aircraft, predating the KC-135 Stratotanker by some three years. A belly-mounted hose-reel assembly was employed to transfer fuel, the receiver aircraft in this case being the sole YB-47F. Like the KB-47G, the YB-47F (0009) was a modified B-47B, being fitted with a nose-mounted probe
(via David Ostrowski)

LEFT
The only Stratojet ever to don the national insignia of a country other than the USA was the specimen loaned to Canada for use in testing the 20,000-lb st (9090-kg st) Orenda Iroquois turbojet engine during the 1950s. Operated by Canadair and known by them as the CL-52, this featured a seventh engine mounted on the starboard fuselage side, it being particularly evident in this approach study. The aircraft concerned was originally manufactured as B-47B-25-BW 12059, being given the identity 'X059' when it acquired Canada's maple leaf markings on wings and fuselage
(via Robert F Dorr)

1956. In turn, the RCAF handed the Stratojet over to Canadair for the necessary modification work which entailed fitting a single 20,000 lb st (9072 kg) Orenda Iroquois jet engine to the starboard aft fuselage.

In fact, several alternative engine locations were studied before the eventual configuration was arrived at, those that were rejected including burial in the fuselage, slinging under the wing and modification of an existing J47 pod. Ultimately, one of the key factors in choosing the aft fuselage location concerned jet blast, it being felt desirable to avoid the hot exhaust efflux impinging on the Stratojet's structure. Careful consideration was also given to engine pod design in order to minimize the detrimental effect on aircraft performance and handling qualities and this ultimately resulted in a measure of area ruling being incorporated in pylon design so as to reduce buffet. Other work entailed reinforcing the fuselage in the vicinity of the engine mounting to tolerate the increased loadings whilst the bomb bay area was extensively modified to accommodate test instrumentation, recording equipment and associated wiring, approximately 100,000 ft (30,480 m) of the latter being involved.

In this form—and in full Canadian military insignia with the RCAF serial number 'X-059'—the CL-52 undertook extensive trials, but all of this work

eventually proved fruitless following cancellation of the impressive Avro Canada CF-105 Arrow, the fighter which the Iroquois engine was ultimately intended to power.

Although produced in substantially greater numbers, the definitive B-47E version of the Stratojet was by no means so prolific with regard to spawning offshoots. Nonetheless, several significant derivatives of the Stratojet family did utilize the standard B-47E airframe as a starting point, some of which—like the EB-47L—were used in only modest numbers for a brief interlude whilst others—most notably the WB-47E—enjoyed a quite lengthy operational career. Seven major sub-types evolved from the B-47E and brief details of these now follow.

YDB-47E/DB-47E At least four aircraft are known to have used the basic DB-47E designation although it appears that these were employed for very different purposes and with a rather different measure of success.

Both of the YDB-47Es (51-5219/220) were associated with the ill-starred GAM-63 Rascal and were probably intended to act as forerunners for a 'production' model for service with the 321st BW at McCoy in a project of rather less ambitious scale than that first intended with the DB-47B (which see). In the event, cancellation of this weapon forestalled operational deployment although it is interesting to note that at least 135 Rascals of three basic sub-types—XGAM-63, GAM-63, and GAM-63A—were ordered between 1951 and 1956.

In addition, two examples of the DB-47E (53-2345/346) are also known to have existed although

Post-production modification of the B-47B model resulted in the appearance of the B-47B-II, this essentially approximating closely to B-47E configuration. Following modification there were few external clues to differentiate between the B-47B-II and the standard B-47E (Boeing via Robert F Dorr)

BELOW
Throughout the course of its career, the Stratojet was employed as an engine test platform on a number of occasions. The example portrayed here on takeoff, B-47B-1-BW 92643, made a significant contribution to the development of the Stratofortress and featured a novel mix of powerplants, the outboard pods being occupied by Pratt & Whitney's J57, variants of which were chosen to power all but the B-52H version of Boeing's massive eight-engined bomber. Inboard pods on this aircraft retained the Stratojet's standard General Electric J47 axial-flow turbojets (via Robert F Dorr)

TOP LEFT
The badge on the nose of this Douglas-built Stratojet and the bulged weapons bay area help to identify it as an EB-47E. Photographed at RAF Brize Norton in Oxfordshire, England, it was assigned to the 301st Bomb Wing, one of two Lockbourne-based wings engaged in electronic countermeasures tasks
(Aviation Photo News)

ABOVE
With the deceleration parachute streaming behind, WB-47E 0-12417 whistles in to land at the end of a weather reconnaissance sortie. The air sampling device which was frequently used by this variant may be seen protruding from the aircraft's belly in the area normally taken up by the bomb bay. One of several types employed by the Air Weather Service's 9th Weather Reconnaissance Group, the WB-47E was likely to be seen anywhere in the world
(Military Aircraft Photographs)

LEFT
Performing 'Reflex Action' duty at RAF Upper Heyford in Oxfordshire, England, from the summer of 1963 until this operation terminated at the end of March 1965, the 509th Bomb Wing is perhaps best known as being the unit which was responsible for dropping the nuclear devices employed against Japan in the final days of World War 2. The Stratojet depicted here on alert at Upper Heyford is a Douglas-built machine and features a blue horizontal arrow near the top of the fin, other squadrons in this wing using white and yellow stripes. Just visible behind and below the wing on 20160 is a 'Tee Town' ECM pod, the 509th BW being one of two units known to have operated aircraft fitted with this equipment
(Aviation Photo News)

these were true to their designation in that they were actually employed as drone directors, probably by the 3205th Drone Group from Eglin AFB, Florida.

EB-47E/EB-47E(TT) As far as the EB-47E is concerned, at least three configurations are known to have existed at different times, these being engaged on various electronic-related tasks.

By far the most numerous were the aircraft employed by SAC's 301st and 376th Bomb Wings from Lockbourne AFB, Ohio, these featuring a bomb-bay capsule containing two EWOs (electronic warfare officers) and a variety of ECM equipment that was intended to confuse and disrupt enemy defensive capability in the event of SAC being committed to combat.

Configurations seem to have varied greatly and these aircraft were almost certainly updated from time to time as more sophisticated ECM became available. The precise nature of the equipment installed in these aircraft was a fairly closely guarded secret and, indeed, there seems to have been a certain amount of obfuscation with regard to their precise designation, many authoritative sources alluding to a variant known as the 'E-47' during the early sixties.

With the benefit of hindsight, it is now clear that this nomenclature actually referred to the EB-47E as employed by the Lockbourne-based units. In the event of war, they would have been employed to 'run interference' for other SAC combat echelons, utilizing the on-board ECM gear to jam enemy radars and thus increase the survivability of bombers intent on penetrating Soviet airspace.

Another EB-47E variant was that employed by

Detachment Four of the 55th SRW from Incirlik, Turkey, as part of Project Iron Work. Known as the EB-47E(TT), this, too, featured a bomb-bay capsule containing two EWOs or 'Ravens', but the 'Tell-Two' Stratojet was a very different beast to the 'standard' SAC EB-47E—it carried a rather more complex array of electronic equipment to monitor Soviet activity at the space centre at Tyuratam and, probably, at the IRBM (intermediate range ballistic missile) test facility at Kapustin Yar. Again, configurations varied amongst the three aircraft which bore this designation, at least one featuring a 'towel-rail' type of antenna on either side of the nose section ahead of the cockpit and another is known to have carried prominent fore and aft SLAR fairings.

The third EB-47E version which has been identified claimed the distinction of being the last Stratojet model to fly regularly in a near-operational capacity and served with the US Navy's Fleet Electronic Warfare Support Group (FEWSG), undertaking trials of ECM-related equipment and also acting as ECM 'aggressors' in Fleet exercises. Two such aircraft existed, both being former 376th BW machines and both carried a variety of ECM gear, some of which was housed in underwing pods. Normally stationed at Tulsa, Oklahoma, they fulfilled this task from 1965, frequently going 'on the road' and visiting major Navy bases in the continental USA until they were eventually replaced by two suitably modified NKC-135A Stratotankers in 1977 and presumably scrapped. In Navy service, the Stratojets carried modified serial numbers, ex-USAF 52-410 becoming '24100' whilst ex-USAF 52-412 became '24120'.

JB-47E Utilized by a small number of B-47Es (and, almost certainly, other examples of the Stratojet) at various times, this designation indicates that a particular aircraft has been temporarily assigned to test duties, such machines usually, though by no means always, reverting to the standard designation upon completion of the project concerned. One example of the Stratojet known to have used the JB-47E designation was 20389 of the Wright Air Research and Development Center at Wright-Patterson AFB, Ohio. However, the nature of the task on which it was engaged is not known.

One of just three Stratojets known to have been operated by the US Navy, NB-47E 0-32104 was assigned to engine test duties when this photograph was taken at Edwards AFB, California, in June 1971. Clearly visible at about the mid-span position beneath the port wing is a seventh engine, the powerplant concerned being an early production example of General Electric's TF34-GE-2 turbofan which was eventually utilized by the Lockheed S-3A Viking
(via Robert F Dorr)

Soaking up the California sunshine at its home base at McClellan, 55th Weather Reconnaissance Squadron WB-47E 0-12417 awaits its next sortie. Amongst the most widely travelled Stratojets, WB-47Es were likely to be seen at almost any location where the USAF maintained a sizeable presence or where it had a particular interest in weather phenomena
(via Robert F Dorr)

LEFT
Originally manufactured by Boeing (Wichita) as a B-47E-55-BW, 12362 was later modified to WB-47E configuration for weather reconnaissance duty with the Military Air Transport Service's Air Weather Service. It is seen here, with others of its kind, in storage at Davis-Monthan AFB, Arizona, during November 1969 and had been scrapped by 1973
(Lindsay Peacock)

NB-47E Allocated to aircraft assigned to permanent test functions, the 'N' prefix was probably applied to several Stratojets over the years, although only one example of an NB-47E has been positively identified. This was 32104, which served as an engine test bed for the Lockheed S-3A Viking programme during the seventies, and it was one of only two seven-engined Stratojets, the other being Canadair's CL-52. Fitted with a single example of the General Electric TF34-GE-2 turbofan at about the mid-span point of the port wing, it was also noteworthy in carrying Navy titles. Unlike the other US Navy Stratojets, however, it retained its full USAF serial number, complete with 'o for obsolete' prefix.

ETB-47E This designation was applied to an unknown number of standard B-47Es modified to perform electronic crew training duties during the fifties.

WB-47E Following on from the solitary and splendidly colourful WB-47B, the WB-47E was rather more numerous and enjoyed a lengthy career with the MATS Air Weather Service, the last examples being retired at the beginning of the seventies. A total of 34 standard B-47Es was converted to this configuration, these for a time also being referred to as W-47Es.

Employed on global weather reconnaissance, the WB-47E featured a variety of sensors to gather such weather-related data as wind velocity and direction, ambient temperature and pressure. Occasionally, they were also used to collect air samples for analysis with a special pod mounted in the position formerly occupied by the bomb bay.

Routine missions took the WB-47Es all over the world and they were also regularly employed to reconnoitre a specific route to be taken by fighters deploying overseas, aspects of duty which conspired to make them some of the hardest-worked of all the 2,000-plus Stratojets, many having logged well in excess of 6,000 flying hours by the time they were eventually withdrawn from use.

In operational service, the WB-47E was only one of several types assigned to the 9th Weather Reconnaissance Group/Wing which maintained squadrons and detachments at various ConUS and overseas bases, WB-47Es being permanently situated at Hunter AFB, Georgia (53rd WRS), and McClellan AFB, California (55th WRS). In addition to these permanent sites, WB-47Es operated regularly from other facilities on a TDY basis.

YB-47J Another particularly rare version of the Stratojet, the YB-47J was essentially a B-47E modified to test the MA.2 radar bombing/navigation attack system earmarked for installation in the larger B-52 Stratofortress. Unfortunately, the identity of the aircraft concerned is not known.

EB-47L At the start of the sixties, when Soviet ICBMs began to present a threat to the survival of SAC's ground-based headquarters, the Command began to direct its attentions towards developing a practical means of ensuring that command and control of its various deterrent forces could still be exercised effectively. One manifestation of this was the 'Looking Glass' airborne command post which began continuous operations in February 1961 and which is still going strong at the time of writing, almost 25 years later.

However, it soon became apparent that the size of the SAC force required expansion of the airborne command elements, additional auxiliary airborne command posts being established at the three bases which hosted numbered Air Force headquarters elements during the spring of 1962. Subsequently, in the summer of that year, SAC also created four Support Squadrons to provide communications relay services, and these were eventually equipped with the EB-47L version of the Stratojet, a total of 35 B-47Es being brought to this configuration in 1962-63, modification work including fitment of the ITT AN/ATC-1 airborne switchboard.

However, with the Stratojet due for a fairly early phase-out, the EB-47L enjoyed only a relatively brief career in the Post Attack Command and Control System (PACCS), its demise almost certainly being accelerated by the realization that suitably modified KC-135As would be far better suited to this task. They could accommodate rather more in the way of communications equipment and provided a much better working environment. Consequently, the EB-47L disappeared from the scene during the opening months of 1965 after a service career lasting barely two years.

As well as those modifications made to the pure bomber variants of the Stratojet, both the RB-47E and RB-47H provided a basis for other sub-types at various times. However, in these instances, the number of aircraft affected was small, but despite the fact that fewer than 20 Stratojets were involved they are nevertheless worthy of some attention.

JRB-47E Another temporary test designation, this was applied to at least one example of the RB-47E, the aircraft concerned (34262) being assigned to the Rome Air Research and Development Center at Griffiss AFB, New York, during the latter half of the fifties. Precisely what the nature of its test duties were remains unclear but it was a much modified machine, featuring a rather deeper and definitely non-standard radome beneath the forward fuselage, an antenna housing on the centre fuselage section more or less adjacent to the leading edge of the wing, a long nose probe and, most interesting of all, long and slender tubular-section cylinders on both sides of the fuselage, these extending aft from a point just ahead of the forward main undercarriage doors. SAC insignia and cannon armament was initially retained,

TOP

With the exception of what appears to be an extra window on the port nose section, B-47E-95-BW 2514 was, in terms of physical appearance, a standard aircraft. Assigned to the Wright Air Development Center when this photograph was taken, it carries the badge of the Air Research and Development Command as well as the inscription The Jet Streamers, *and could conceivably have been engaged in evaluating the effects of high altitude winds on aircraft performance*
(*via Robert F Dorr*)

ABOVE

Disposition of the Stratojet fleet began at quite an early stage, the first examples to be committed to storage being mainly RB-47E models made redundant by a reduction in the size of SAC's reconnaissance force. One rather unusual Stratojet which had found its way to Davis-Monthan by April 1960 was the aircraft seen here. Previously assigned to the Air Research and Development Command's Rome Air Development Center, JRB-47E 34262 was one of the first aircraft to be scrapped
(*Douglas Olson via Philip Chinnery*)

TOP LEFT
Photographed while serving with the Aeronautical Systems Division at Wright-Patterson AFB, Ohio, B-47E 0-32104 features an unusual bomb bay modification, a rather prominent bulge being visible in this area. The nature of this modification remains a mystery but this aircraft later went on to be one of the last airworthy Stratojets, operating under Navy auspices for several years and being instrumental in development of the Lockheed S-3A Viking anti-submarine warfare aircraft

ABOVE
Its engine test career over, NB-47E 0-32104 ultimately found its way to Davis-Monthan AFB, Arizona for long-term storage, being photographed there in March 1975, soon after arrival. One of the last Stratojets to enter the 'bone yard', it was also one of the few to escape, eventually being transferred to a museum collection in Colorado
(via Robert F Dorr)

LEFT
Another Wright-Patterson based aircraft, B-47E 0-32280 features the Aeronautical Systems Division's dayglo fin stripe as well as the Air Force Systems Command badge on the nose section. During the course of a test career which spanned several years, this Stratojet participated in several different projects
(via John Hughes)

The penultimate RB-47E, 0-34263, was eventually modified to drone configuration as a JQB-47E, surviving its period of use as a target to meet its demise at the hands of the breakers at Davis-Monthan AFB, Arizona in the early 1970s. Featuring rather faded dayglo paint and the Air Force Systems Command badge, it was one of only two Stratojet drones known to have entered storage (Douglas Olson via Philip Chinnery)

LEFT

Arguably one of the most bizarre colour schemes ever applied to any Stratojet was that worn by what appears to be a B-47E, the wings, tailplane, fuselage and fin being brightly decorated with alternating red and white stripes while photo reference marks were also applied to the starboard side in the vicinity of the cockpit and aft fuselage sections. Small size service inscriptions would seem to indicate that this finish was carried in the early 1950s but the precise reason for these rather garish markings remains obscure, as does the identity of the aircraft concerned (via Philip Chinnery)

although by the time this aircraft was retired this had been deleted, the nose probe also having been removed.

JQB-47E/QB-47E Arguably the most colourful—and, certainly, the most visible—of all the Stratojets by virtue of the liberal application of fluorescent dayglo paint, some 14 RB-47Es were eventually modified to drone configuration and used as targets in the development of missiles such as the Boeing IM-99 Bomarc.

Two 'prototype' conversions were employed to prove that such a large aircraft could be successfully operated in this way, these being followed by 12 'production' examples, all 14 apparently being operated by the 3205th Drone Group from Eglin AFB, Florida. The process of conversion entailed fitment of radio control equipment which permitted the aircraft to be 'flown' remotely, control during the critical takeoff and landing regimes being exercised by an operator on an MRW-5A vehicle. Once safely airborne, management of the QB-47E was 'handed-off' to a suitably-configured drone director aircraft such as the DB-47E.

Other modification work included the provision of an arrester hook behind the aft main gear member, this being used to bring the aircraft to a halt following an unmanned flight. The QB-47E also carried special wing pods, each of which contained six 16-mm movie cameras to record data relating to missile testing. In addition, it seems certain that explosive self-destruct charges were also carried, these being primed to detonate automatically after a certain interval in the event of control being lost whilst in flight or following command instruction from the drone director aircraft

Oblique radar mapping and the monitoring of radio and radar emissions were apparently the primary tasks of the ERB-47H model, such as 36245 depicted here. Taken from standard RB-47H production, the three aircraft involved featured numerous bumps and bulges and carried a crew of five, unlike the RB-47H which accommodated a six-man crew. Mission specialists were housed in the bulged bomb bay area which contained a pressurized capsule and, like all H models, these aircraft were assigned to the 55th Strategic Reconnaissance Wing
(Boeing via Philip Chinnery)

BELOW
The last RB-47H to be retired by SAC's 55th Strategic Reconnaissance Wing, 0-34296 was destined to spend only a brief interlude at the Military Aircraft Storage and Disposition Center at Davis-Monthan. Upon its return to flying duties it spent several years at Los Angeles Air Force Station and was closely associated with testing of F-111 avionics systems, hence the 'needle nose'. It was also unique in being the only RB-47H ever to feature white undersides. With test flying over, it found its way to Eglin AFB, Florida, where it may still be seen today
(Aviation Photo News)

in instances of erratic behaviour. Routine unmanned 'Nullo' flights would have taken the 'Q-planes' over the nearby Gulf of Mexico which has, over the years, become the last resting place for several hundred drones of various types.

In practice, cost considerations dictated that the QB-47Es were not initially viewed as expendable targets, for they were hugely expensive when compared with other types of drone. Accordingly, missiles were invariably programmed to make near misses but there were, almost inevitably, 'accidents'. At least one QB-47E was destroyed by a Bomarc which succeeded in scoring a direct hit on the unfortunate Stratojet. Most of the QB-47Es eventually met their demise during the course of missile test work but at least two survived to be placed in storage at Davis-Monthan where they were eventually scrapped.

Interestingly, both were designated JQB-47Es at the time of their retirement, one displaying a total of seven silhouettes on the port nose section which provided tantalising clues of the type of work undertaken. One of the silhouettes clearly depicted a Bomarc missile, whilst three more bore a strong resemblance to the Lockheed SR-71—these were meant to depict the YF-12A which, had it been procured for service with the USAF's Air Defense Command, would have utilized the Hughes AIM-47A long-range air-to-air missile. It seems reasonable to assume that this Stratojet (34256) participated in a series of live-firing trials as part of the process of verifying the YF-12's Hughes AN/ASG-18 radar and the closely associated AIM-47 weapon during the early to mid-sixties.

ERB-47H Another variant assigned specifically to the task of gathering electronic intelligence, the ERB-47H served solely with the 55th SRW and appears to have spent most of its operational career with Detachment Four at Incirlik in Turkey, although they were sporadic visitors to Brize Norton and Upper Heyford and may well have accomplished part of their designated task from these two RAF bases.

All three were taken from the final batch of Stratojets to be acquired by the USAF, RB-47Hs 36245, 36246 and 36249 being the three machines involved but it is not known whether modification was accomplished on the production line or at a later date in their service career which lasted until at least May 1967 when one was noted at Upper Heyford. The precise nature of their mission remains undefined—as, indeed, does their avionics fit—but there is evidence to support the belief that they were engaged on oblique radar mapping and it is known that these aircraft employed a five-man crew consisting of pilot, copilot, navigator and two electronic warfare officers, the latter occupying a compartment in the aircraft's belly.

Chapter 6
The Stratojet Aloft

As far as flying the Stratojet was concerned, it seems to have been very much a case of this being one of those types which didn't suffer fools gladly. Most published accounts tend to confirm that it could be unforgiving and given the right (or wrong, depending on one's proximity to the aircraft in question) circumstances, this was definitely one machine that could kill.

Certainly, it seems to have had a distressing tendency to avenge itself on anyone who took liberties, but even those who always played it pretty close to the rule book could come unstuck from time to time, there being many pitfalls waiting to snare the unwary. As a consequence, it would probably be fair to say that pilots tended to develop a love-hate relationship with the Stratojet. Many loved it and many hated it, while, regardless of their own personal viewpoint, most seem to have treated it with respect.

The root cause of many of the problems likely to be encountered stemmed from the fact that the Stratojet never possessed a surfeit of power, despite being fitted with six engines and despite the amount of available thrust virtually doubling during the course of the aircraft's production life. Weight growth saw to that, more than swallowing up any benefits likely to accrue from extra thrust. There is no doubt that, towards the end of its operational career with SAC, the B-47 was definitely underpowered. This lack of power could, and frequently did, have dire consequences for the crew in the event of, for example, an outboard engine failure on a heavyweight departure. It is hardly surprising that confidence in the Stratojet tended to diminish as it inexorably put on weight. Rather like an ageing woman, its allure diminished as it gained avoirdupois.

The unusual undercarriage configuration also caused problems from time to time, instances of weathercocking or porpoising periodically culminating in disaster and, indeed, during the first few years

of service close to half of all B-47 accidents occurred on landing.

In case all of the foregoing tends to induce a belief that the Stratojet was a killer, let me hasten to add that this was not so. If flown correctly, the B-47 was safe, although it is probably true to say that there were more potential hazards than on other contemporary types. Certainly, though, the Stratojet was no more or less likely to succumb to Newton's law than any other aircraft in the hands of a skilled and well-trained pilot who was familiar with its foibles.

Following the usual planning and pre-flight inspection, a typical B-47 mission would begin with departure for the active runway and, since the Stratojet consumed fuel at a fairly prodigious rate whilst on the ground—approximately 150–200 lb (68–91 kg) per min was typical, this equating to one minute of cruise at normal operational altitude—it was obviously desirable to get airborne with the minimum delay.

As already noted, takeoff was one of the more critical moments, demanding careful attention to weight and balance calculations to ensure that enough runway was available. In the continental USA, where 10,000-ft (3048-m) runways were the norm, there was usually a reasonable margin for error, unlike the

Ten B-47Bs, seven KC-97s, three B-25s, two C-45s and single examples of the C-47, C-54, and C-82 are visible in this study of March Air Force Base's flight line in the mid-1950s. In the foreground, control tower personnel check 'flight strips' relating to the day's activity, while close study of the B-47s reveals subtle variations in colour schemes. This scene would have been re-enacted at roughly a score of USAF air bases at this time
(Joe Bruch via Paul Bennett)

overseas bases where space was often at a premium. Even then, in certain states—Florida, Louisiana, Texas, and Arizona are good examples—it was frequently necessary to operate at restricted gross weights during the summer months for, with just 36,000-lb (16,329-kg) of dry thrust available, the B-47 was not noted for outstanding performance in the acceleration stakes.

Water-alcohol injection did increase sea level thrust quite substantially, to around the 43,000-lb (19,504-kg) mark, but this method of thrust augmentation was generally avoided for routine operations since frequent use necessitated modification to the trailing edge and flaps. In the UK, though, redeploying B-47s invariably employed water injection on takeoff.

As far as RATO was concerned, cost consciousness played no small part in the decision to restrict this to the status of an emergency measure which would mainly be used to ensure that alert-dedicated and nuclear-armed aircraft would get airborne promptly in the event of the EWO (emergency war order) being transmitted. Harking back to the UK again, it appears that mission-ready B-47s would have been unable to takeoff without recourse to RATO, while there is, apparently, good reason to believe that in our all too rare hot summers even RATO augmentation would not have been sufficient to propel a fully-laden Stratojet into the sky. In such circumstances, 'Reflex Action' bombers would have been removed from alert but whether this ever actually happened is not known.

Another restraint on use of RATO centred around disposal of the bottles once they had burned out. While most local residents might have adopted a fairly fatalistic attitude with regard to the presence of nuclear bombers at a nearby base, they would certainly not have relished the prospect of being 'bombed' by exhausted RATO racks deposited by Stratojets engaged on routine training missions. As a result, RATO was used only rarely.

Consequently, with only 'dry' thrust available, a fully loaded Stratojet would require something in the region of three miles of runway to get airborne from a field some 2,000 ft (610 m) above sea level when the

Close study of the data panel which appears on the nose of 320th Bomb Wing Stratojet 12237 reveals that post-production modification has resulted in a change of designation from B-47B-40-BW to B-47B-I-47-BW. This machine, like the other half a dozen aircraft visible in the background, features white anti-flash paint on the undersurfaces. In the left foreground, the Stratojet's crew discuss the forthcoming sortie before gathering up their personal kit—parachutes, helmets, and 'secrets'—and boarding the Stratojet
(Boeing via Philip Chinnery)

temperature was hovering at about the 80 degree mark. In view of that, it was hardly surprising that heavyweight departures were most definitely not the order of the day at certain bases during the summer months.

Even assuming that the crew had performed their calculations correctly, other factors such as a wet runway, tailwind or low engine EGT (exhaust gas temperature) could still have a potentially hazardous effect on field performance. One of the key equations in any B-47 takeoff was 'critical field length', which was essentially the distance needed to accelerate at a given weight to a specific speed for takeoff, even allowing for the loss of one engine or, alternatively, abort with sufficient space left to come to a safe halt before running out of concrete.

Needless to say, things could still go disastrously wrong for this calculation failed to take into account the possibility of braking chute failure, tyre bursts or hesitation on the part of the pilot and this was partly responsible for one other important figure being worked out for every takeoff. This was the so-called 'line speed', which essentially referred to the speed at which the B-47 should have been moving as it passed the 2,500-ft (762-m) mark. Enabling crew members to establish whether or not their aircraft was accelerating at the desired rate and, ultimately, whether it was safe to proceed with the takeoff run, this no doubt helped to avoid many accidents.

One other aspect of the takeoff procedure which deserves mention was introduced after the B-47 had been in service for several years when the threat posed by Soviet ICBMs greatly reduced the amount of reaction time to launch SAC's huge bomber force. SAC responded with the MITO (minimum interval takeoff) concept. Like most changes in operational

procedure, it was exhaustively evaluated by SAC before being accepted as part of normal doctrine.

Initially, fears that the amount of exhaust smoke and turbulence generated by the B-47—or, for that matter, any large aircraft—would prove hazardous conspired to limit the acceptable interval between aircraft to one minute.

Project 'Open Road' changed all that. It arose out of a series of tests conducted at Edwards AFB, California, which revealed that the degree of difficulty inherent in close-interval departures was somewhat overstated. Accordingly, SAC started its own evaluation which was accomplished during 1959–60 under the code name Open Road. Essentially, this entailed gradual reduction of the time lag between aircraft and by the time the exploratory phase was completed in January 1960 B-47s were routinely departing at intervals of just 15 seconds in perfect safety.

Obviously, the introduction of MITO signally affected other aspects of operational procedure and it became normal for final pre-flight checks to be undertaken whilst taxying so that the aircraft could apply full power and commence its take-off as soon as it reached the end of the active runway.

Since MITO was intended to facilitate the rapid departure of alert-dedicated aircraft, water injection was regularly used. This did of course result in large amounts of smoke being deposited, which greatly reduced visibility for those taking-off later in the stream. To overcome this problem and provide a measure of guidance, two white lines were painted on the runway—one on the left half and one on the right half—departing bombers alternating between these.

Terminating in January 1960, the lessons learned in Open Road were applied on a fleet-wide basis soon

Displaying the badge of the 307th Bomb Wing on the nose section, B-47E-120-BW 32342 taxies towards the runway at RAF Greenham Common in Berkshire, England, during a routine alert exercise in the early 1960s. Such events were fairly frequent occurrences, the alert force firing up and running through normal pre-departure procedures up to the point of reaching the runway. Once there, they invariably returned to dispersal to resume alert duty. Normally resident at Lincoln AFB, Nebraska, the 307th BW furnished aircraft for 'Reflex Action' at Greenham Common from August 1962 until June 1963 when it gave way to the 384th BW from Little Rock (Aviation Photo News)

BELOW
B-47E 32104 gets airborne in what seems to have been a fairly clean departure. Stratojets redeploying from UK SAC bases invariably seemed to have done their best to black out local areas, thick clouds of pungent smoke being accompanied by an often painful noise level (McDonnell Douglas via Robert F Dorr)

afterwards and MITO quickly became routine, being extended to encompass the larger eight-engined B-52 force as well as KC-97 and KC-135 tankers. Indeed, tests involving these types witnessed the launch of six KC-97s in just 59 seconds while five B-52s managed to get airborne in 68 seconds.

Today, a quarter of a century later, MITO remains standard operating procedure and anyone who has ever witnessed such a departure by a cell of B-52s or KC-135s will readily acknowledge that it is an impressive, smoky and almost painfully noisy spectacle.

Having once got airborne—which, despite the foregoing, tended to happen rather more often than not—and cleaned up the aircraft, it was usual to initiate a rapid climb to altitude where the jet engine functions rather more efficiently, power settings being maintained at or close to the 100 per cent mark. Rate of climb varied according to payload, light-weight Stratojets achieving a fairly impressive initial rate of about 4,000 ft (1220 m) per min and usually averaging about 2,500 ft (762 m) per min throughout. Corresponding figures for heavyweight aircraft were

*Featuring the original
natural metal overall
finish, B-47B-25-BW
12071 cruises above the
clouds. The small
'United States Air
Force' legend beneath
the cockpit is
noteworthy, this method
of presentation being
abandoned in favour of
larger 'U.S. Air Force'
inscriptions during the
course of the 1950s*
(Boeing via Philip
Chinnery)

of the order of 2,000 and 1,300 ft (610–396 m) per min respectively.

In the early days at least, when the Stratojet was still considered to be immune to the threat posed by interceptors and/or surface-to-air missiles, much of the time was spent at fairly high altitude. Since the B-47's unrefuelled radius of action was at best only modest, it was usual to establish a cruise pattern aimed at bestowing the greatest possible range. Accordingly, aircraft normally climbed immediately to whatever altitude was calculated to be optimum for a specific weight whereupon flight at a constant Mach number followed.

Ideally, the aircraft was then allowed to 'cruise-climb' as fuel burned off although in certain training areas, such as those where traffic was dense and where it was essential for aircraft to fly at specific altitudes, it was more common to employ what was referred to as a 'step climb'. Whilst having a slightly deleterious effect on range, this technique was much safer for all concerned since air traffic controllers knew precisely where the aircraft was. At least, that was the theory...

In the step climb, the autopilot's altitude hold mode was normally engaged which had the effect of causing the B-47 to maintain a constant height. But, as the Stratojet's weight decreased, so its speed rose and when this occurred it was usual to disengage the autopilot for a few moments while the aircraft sought a new and more appropriate level for the desired constant Mach number. Where traffic was particularly heavy, it became necessary to compromise and in such instances a planned step climb with longer 'steps' was undertaken. This, naturally, also affected range but the impact was not great and with safety considerations paramount the sacrifice was felt to be justified.

Most missions also included at least one in-flight refuelling rendezvous and whilst few pilots became so blasé as to be dismissive of the hazards inherent in putting two large aircraft into close proximity in space there is no doubt that it was viewed largely as a routine activity and one which for old hands was 'no sweat'. However, the fact that the B-47 was good in formation did tend to make life a little bit easier.

Refuelling normally took place at medium altitude—somewhere around the 20,000 ft (6096 m) mark when taking fuel from a piston-engined KC-97 and anything from five to ten thousand feet higher when the tanker was the jet-powered KC-135A—so it was almost always necessary for the bomber aircraft to descend in order to effect a rendezvous. With vastly different performance figures, techniques varied according to which type of tanker was to furnish fuel but it seems that the ideal airspeed was of the order of 255 knots (472 km/h). This meant that it sometimes became necessary to adopt the so-called 'toboggan' technique when in contact with a KC-97, both aircraft setting up a descending flight path during the course of fuel transfer.

Regardless of which type of aircraft was dispensing fuel, the bomber pilot could not afford to relax. He had to continue to fine-tune his aircraft to maintain contact. This, by the way, did not mean that the copilot was just along for the ride. Indeed, the latter's task was probably no less important. He had to ensure that the incoming fuel found its way into the correct tanks in the correct order, the B-47 being highly susceptible to centre of gravity problems since virtually all of its fuel was accommodated longitudinally in the fuselage.

Even though the mid to late-fifties was a period when the fuel budget was seemingly inexhaustible, it was nevertheless in SAC's interest to obtain the best value possible from any sortie. Accordingly, most missions also incorporated other routine training objectives to permit crews to polish their skills and, ideally, attain a level of ability in which the various disciplines involved in the strategic bombing task were what might best be described as second nature. Such objectives were many and varied but notable examples include bombing, navigation and, following the decision to introduce greatly revised penetration techniques from late in that decade, sustained flight at low level. Any combination—or, indeed, all—could be encountered during the course of a training sortie.

As far as the former was concerned, radar bomb scoring (RBS) enabled the Command to establish a crew's skill—or lack of it—in putting bombs on target without it actually being necessary for them to physically release any weapons. It was a most cost effective method since it was relatively inexpensive to operate. Further benefit accrued from the fact that it was also a mobile system which meant that the designated target could be moved almost at will, greatly compounding the degree of reality and, as a by-product, eliminating the possibility of familiarity breeding contempt on the part of the crew called upon to carry out an 'attack'. As a result, SAC's RBS equipment was likely to be deployed almost anywhere and many of the great cities of the USA were 'destroyed' by bombers operating by day or night against an RBS site.

Introduced to service as long ago as 1946, when the first RBS site in San Diego logged 888 'bomb releases', use of this training aid quickly expanded and it is still very much a part of contemporary SAC operations, more than 100,000 RBS runs being accomplished annually. Essentially, it relies on a combination of radio and radar in determining the accuracy of a simulated attack, ground-based scoring radars locking-on to an approaching bomber and tracking it automatically on a plotting board. On the bomber itself—be it a B-36, B-47, B-52 or FB-111—radio equipment begins to transmit a tone signal to the scoring facility as it nears the 'target', this tone ceasing at the moment of weapon 'release', thus permitting RBS personnel to determine the bomber's position relative to the target at the relevant moment. Subsequent calculations—taking into account such

Portrayed against a snow-shrouded and heavily forested backdrop, the clean lines of the XB-47 prototype are all too apparent in this study. At a later date, the addition of underwing tanks and installation of mission-related electronic equipment did much to mar the Stratojet's elegant appearance but they never completely succeeded in disguising its aesthetic qualities
(via Robert F Dorr)

LEFT
The first of many. Lacking identifying titles, XB-47 prototype 6065 accelerates for takeoff during the early stages of its flight test career. Sadly, this historically-significant aircraft did not survive but the second prototype can still be seen today at Chanute AFB, Illinois, albeit in bogus markings
(via Robert F Dorr)

BOTTOM LEFT
Resplendent in white anti-flash undersurfaces, B-47B-II 12336 was one of a large number of early production Stratojets which were retrospectively updated to near B-47E standard. Evidence of stress wrinkles may just be discerned on the fuselage sides beneath the leading edge of the wing
(via Philip Chinnery)

BELOW
The last unit to perform 'Reflex Action' at Greenham Common was the 301st Bomb Wing from Lockbourne AFB, Ohio, their EB-47Es being present at this base for about two months leading up to the end of Greenham's 'Reflex' commitment on 31 May 1964. Sharply outlined by black smoke rising from a routine fire practice, 31963 was typical of the EB-47Es present throughout this period
(John Hughes)

TOP
B-47E 32102 of the 384th BW at Little Rock AFB,
Arkansas sits at dispersal at Greenham Common while
undergoing 'Reflex Action' ground alert duty in July 1963.
Clearly visible beneath the aft fuselage is the RATO
installation, this particular specimen being fitted with 20
bottles
(John Hughes)

Lack of tail gun armament and auxiliary fuel tanks help to
identify this particular Stratojet as one of the handful of
aircraft employed by the 3920th Combat Support Group
on continuity training and general support duties.
Normally resident at Brize Norton, the 3920th's B-47Es,
like 0-20518, were frequently sighted at all the UK SAC
bases
(John Hughes)

With the full 30-bottle RATO installation, EB-47E 32127 of the 301st Bomb Wing sits out its three-week spell of alert duty at Brize Norton in 1964. The bulged bomb-bay area and additional protuberances beneath the aft fuselage confirm that this was one of a fairly large number of 301st and 376th BW Stratojets assigned to electronic countermeasures duties
(John Hughes)

Liberally daubed with high-visibility dayglo, the QB-47Es must surely have ranked as being amongst the most colourful of all the Stratojets. Assigned to the Air Force Systems Command's 3205th Drone Group, they operated from Eglin AFB, Florida during the early 1960s. This example, O-34256, was one of two known to have been consigned to storage at Davis-Monthan AFB, Arizona
(Lindsay Peacock)

LEFT
One of just three Stratojets used by the US Navy, NB-47E 0-32104 was committed for storage in 1975, eventually finding its way to a museum collection in Colorado during 1979. Whilst in Navy service, it played a key part in testing the Lockheed S-3A's General Electric TF34 engine
(Ray Leader)

BOTTOM LEFT
Another survivor and one of the last airworthy examples of the Stratojet, RB-47H 0-34296 was closely involved in avionics trials associated with the General Dynamics F-111, being assigned to the 6592nd Air Base Group at Los Angeles during the early 1970s. Unique in being the only RB-47H ever to fly with white undersides, it presently resides at Eglin AFB, Florida where it was photographed in 1979 with a hybrid nose cone taken from B-47E 15251
(Stephen Miller)

BELOW
Preserved at the Oklahoma City State Fairground, B-47E 0-12387 is one of only a modest number of survivors as well as being amongst the most eye-catching by virtue of being displayed in flying attitude. Remarkably, it keeps company with a B-52 which is mounted in similar fashion
(Geoffrey Rhodes)

The end of the line. The last Stratojets to be employed by the USAF in an operational capacity were the WB-47Es of the Air Weather Service which remained active until the dawn of the 1970s. Like most B-47s, they ended up at Davis-Monthan, 0-12362 being seen there in November 1969 shortly after arrival
(Lindsay Peacock)

criteria as distance, direction, aircraft speed, heading, altitude, wind and ballistics characteristics of the weapon being simulated—enable ground-based technicians to establish precisely where the impact point would have been had a bomb or string of bombs actually been delivered.

As already noted, training missions generally included at least one simulated attack but it was not uncommon for multiple attacks to be made, with aircraft approaching from a different direction, simulating the use of various types of weapon and, last but by no means least, practising alternative means of delivery.

RBS also played an important part in the command-wide SAC bombing competition which was usually held on an annual basis and in which the B-47 participated during the period from 1953 to 1965. Initial showings by Stratojet-equipped Bomb Wings were poor and it was not until 1955 that the 320th BW emerged victorious when it secured the prestigious Fairchild Trophy, awarded to the unit posting the best score in the combined fields of bombing and navigation. Subsequently, during the three years from 1957 to 1959, the Stratojet reigned supreme in competition for the Fairchild Trophy, the 321st BW, 306th BW and 307th BW being successive winners.

Cancelled during 1962 to 1964 as a result of heavy operational commitments and cost considerations, the competition was resumed in 1965, this being the last year in which the Stratojet took part. Plattsburgh's 380th SAW came out top of the five B-47 units involved but was unable to match the performance put up by *Miss Magnolia*—a B-52F of the 454th BW—which returned to Columbus, Mississippi, with the Fairchild Trophy. By the time of the 1966 competition, the B-47 was history, having disappeared from the bomber inventory early in February of that year.

As far as bombing was concerned, the early years of the Stratojet's career, when the type was considered to be more or less immune to interception, were mostly spent at altitude and it was here that the phenomenon known as 'coffin corner' awaited, this being more correctly referred to as the aerodynamic ceiling or, in more simple terms, the point at which low-speed stall and high-speed buffet coincide.

When 'coffin corner' was encountered, normal recovery measures were ineffective since the aircraft would quite literally stall due to both lack of speed and surfeit of speed. Consequently, if one pulled back on the control column to slow the aircraft one would enter slow-speed stall and if one pushed forward on the control column to gain speed one would enter the compressibility stall regime and both could, to use modern idiom, 'ruin one's day'. Fortunately, the rules of aerodynamics permitted the location of 'coffin corner' to be determined precisely, and once aware of just where the danger lurked it was a relatively easy matter to avoid.

For a B-47 operating at a weight of 200,000 lb (90,718 kg), the 'coffin corner' phenomenon would be encountered at Mach 0.75 at 36,000 ft (10,973 m), this being several thousand feet above the best cruise altitude which fortuitously provided a handsome margin for error. As weight decreased, so the 'coffin corner' rose and for a 120,000-lb (54,431-kg) Stratojet cruising at Mach 0.75 it was of the order of 45,000 ft (13,716-m), which was still some 6,000 ft (1829 m) or so above the optimum cruise level. With such margins, in the normal course of events one clearly had to be almost unbelievably careless to get into trouble although there were some instances of turbulence bringing about a loss of control, most notably when pilots climbed to pass above storm activity. In such cases, when flying close to but below the aerodynamic ceiling, it was possible for a gust-induced slow-speed stall to occur, the problem then being to judge the ensuing recovery correctly and avoid encountering high-speed buffet.

Generally, though, the B-47 was pleasant to fly, and demonstrated an ability to perform aerobatic manoeuvres like loops and rolls at an early date. It was, of course, necessary to exercise great care not to overload the structure and, despite the fact that aerobatics were prohibited by SAC, there were almost inevitably those who occasionally indulged when nobody was looking.

Eventually, following a far-reaching change in tactics, SAC directed that certain manoeuvres should be practised regularly and it was this decision which was largely responsible for several aircraft being destroyed as a result of fatigue failure in the late fifties, this also marking the start of a period when the B-47 could no longer bank on being relatively safe at altitude in the event of being committed to combat. Accordingly, like many other contemporary bombers, it was forced to fly somewhat closer to the ground to increase the likelihood of a successful attack.

Initially, all appears to have gone quite well following the switch to low-level penetration techniques in about 1957–58 but there was one particular method of weapons delivery which did place undue and unacceptable stress on the airframe, this being the LABS (low-altitude bombing system) manoeuvre. Essentially, LABS called for the B-47 to approach the target at very low level before pulling up into a half loop or 'Immelman turn', during which the weapon was released, the bomb being literally 'thrown' at the target. Thereafter, the B-47 half-rolled right side up and departed hastily on a reciprocal heading, having gained several thousand feet of altitude in the meantime, this often being converted to energy during the course of a rapid descent to get back to the relative security of low level.

Another manoeuvre, also designed to enhance the probability of a successful attack, called for the bomber to approach at low level before climbing

TOP LEFT
Progressive modernization of the original production B-47B variant resulted in the advent of the B-47B-I and B-47B-II, both of which approximated closely to B-47E standard. This B-47B, 12336, was one of the aircraft subjected to updating, the most obvious physical difference entailing deletion of the integral RATO installation in favour of the jettisonable 'horse-collar' unit. Some structural strengthening was also undertaken
(Boeing via Philip Chinnery)

ABOVE
A 1,000-aircraft production run is always a milestone worth observing and Boeing duly decorated B-47E-105-BW 2609 in recognition of the fact that it was the 1,000th Stratojet to be completed by the Wichita factory. Delivered to the USAF in December 1954, 2609 began its service career in the original natural metal overall finish and rather unusually featured the Strategic Air Command badge to starboard in the place normally occupied by the badge of the bomb wing of assignment
(Boeing via Michael O'Leary)

LEFT
In the more normal course of events, flying the B-47 seems to have presented few problems, the type apparently possessing few vices when operating at medium altitude. Aircrews did, however, have to beware the so-called 'coffin-corner', this being the point at which slow speed stall and high speed buffet coincide. The subject of this picture, B-47E 32282, is obviously in no danger
(USAF via Robert F Dorr)

rapidly to medium altitude for its bombing run. Once free of its weapon, the bomber would execute a sharp turn away from the target and a rapid descent to get back down 'among the weeds' as quickly as possible.

Needless to say, neither method of attack was terribly difficult to plan and execute but it was quite easy to overload the structure with the consequent risk of disastrous fatigue failure and this is in fact what occurred. Matters came to a head in the spring of 1958 when half-a-dozen examples of the Stratojet crashed in quick succession and the ensuing investigation and inspection revealed a number of areas where fatigue was apparent as well as pinpointing the so-called 'milk bottle pin' as the prime culprit in the recent spate of accidents.

This was essentially the main wing-fuselage attachment fitting and the modification programme aimed at eradicating such failures which ensued was code-named Project Milk Bottle, it being one of the few instances that I can recall of a code-name not being designed to obfuscate. Not surprisingly, incorporating a fix was horrendously expensive although the outlay was perhaps mitigated by the fact that SAC got another six years of service out of the Stratojet while it would be foolish to attempt to place a finite value on the metallurgical lessons learned as a result of this costly episode. Suffice it to say that those responsible for producing large jet aircraft were still somewhat ignorant even at this late date and, like the rather less fortunate early Comet jet airliners, Boeing's Stratojet was truly a pioneer, contributing much valuable data for the aircraft that followed.

To return to our typical mission, following the

change in penetration methods and weapons delivery tactics, sustained flight at low level was regularly undertaken in order to provide crews with experience of handling what was still considered to be a large aircraft in close proximity to the ground.

Virtually all of this training was accomplished over the USA. Despite the fact that vast tracts of land were sparsely populated or totally uninhabited, it was not possible for even such a large country to permit bombers to roam around more or less as they pleased. Consequently, a number of clearly-defined low level areas were established solely for use by SAC aircraft, such tracks originally being known as 'Oil Burner' routes, this presumably alluding to the fact that fuel consumption was significantly greater.

Low level training is still undertaken today although it is now performed on 'Olive Branch' routes, the title being changed in deference to the often-vocal conservation lobby who seem to have mastered the art of overlooking the fact that their continuing security might well one day be dependent on the ability of the military personnel that they so frequently denigrate. Indeed, so dogmatic are they at times, one could very well argue that it is a classic case of not being able to 'see the wood for the trees', if one might be permitted to employ an allegory which is probably close to their hearts.

Sustained low-level operation in any kind of aircraft does, of course, demand great concentration for there are many potential hazards—even a momentary lapse could have fatal consequences. For a start, one has to be alert for obstacles on one's flight path and take the necessary avoiding action and it should not be forgotten that electronic luxuries such as terrain-following radar simply did not exist then. Consequently, it was probably the nearest thing that SAC aircrews got to what might best be described as 'seat of the pants' flying, but in addition to being mentally fatiguing it was almost certainly physically tiring since the amount of energy expended in driving a B-47 around was undoubtedly rather greater than that burned by a fighter pilot. It should also be kept in mind that bomber crews were invariably airborne for rather longer periods of time.

Add to that the fact that the B-47 would transmit what seemed like every shock, bump and jolt of the often turbulent air through to the crew compartment for periods which often exceeded two hours and one will quickly appreciate that crew members earned their flight pay the hard way. One also begins to comprehend why the humble sick bag was such an important piece of flight kit for even the toughest stomach would occasionally rebel when exposed to such harsh treatment for two hours or more.

Assuming that one didn't crash on takeoff, collide with a tanker, fall victim to 'coffin corner' or fly into an obstacle during the low level sector, a 'typical' mission would terminate with let-down, approach and a return to terra firma.

There appear to have been two distinct schools of thought on the let-down procedure, both having their own advantages and disadvantages. Whilst there seems to have been a certain amount of latitude with regard to which method was employed, I suspect that it may not have been quite as simple as that, factors like weather, terrain and proximity to centres of

Aerial refuelling was instrumental in transforming the Stratojet from the status of a medium-range bomber to one that possessed genuine intercontinental capability, another Boeing product, the KC-97 Stratofreighter, being purchased in huge quantities for service with SAC tanker squadrons. This is the view that the boom operator enjoyed when in contact with a Stratojet, the aircraft receiving fuel actually being the very first production B-47B (Boeing via Paul Bennett)

LEFT

Taken from a chase aircraft during the course of inflight refuelling trials, B-47B-1-BW 92642 tops up its tanks from KC-97E 1214 somewhere over the United States. Aerial refuelling was a routine feature of virtually all Stratojet sorties and quickly became second nature to aircrews. Interesting features of this Stratojet are the lack of tail gun armament and the auxiliary fuel tanks mounted between the podded jet engines, while it also has the fixed RATO installation that was a standard feature of the B model. Note also the considerable amount of wing flexing that is evident (Boeing via Paul Bennett)

population probably playing their part in influencing the procedure employed.

Taking the gear-down method first, this was usually initiated at a point about 40 miles from the field and resulted in a fairly constant rate of descent— of the order of 7,000–8,000 ft/min (2134–2438 m)— being maintained throughout. It should be borne in mind that the B-47 lacked spoilers or speed brakes but the undercarriage itself acted as a most efficient airbrake even though the 305-knot (564-km/h) IAS restriction on gear extension did limit the rate of descent somewhat.

If one confined one's calculations solely to the descent phase, the gear-down method was clearly superior on the dual counts of both time and fuel, this method taking six minutes and requiring the expenditure of 310 lb (141 kg) of fuel. However, the equation changed significantly when one took into account the amount of time required and fuel burned from the 70-mile (113-km) point which was normally where a gear-up descent would begin, for the B-47 performing a gear-down descent would consume 450 lb (204 kg) of fuel during the four minutes it took to reach the let-down point.

On the other hand, a clean aircraft, initiating let-down 70 miles (113 km) out, required nine minutes

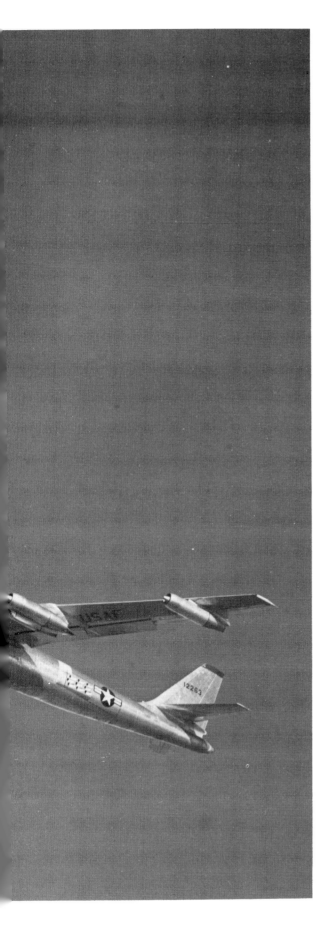

and just 530 lb (240 kg) of fuel to reach the same point in the traffic pattern, but this technique was rather less spectacular during the first four minutes when the rate of descent hovered around the 2,000–3,000 ft/min (610–914 m) mark. Thereafter, the descent curve steepened substantially, peaking at an 'ear-popping' 9,000 ft/min (2743 m) in the seventh minute and never dropping below 5,000 ft/min (1524 m).

A third method that was frequently employed represented something of a compromise but was probably more comfortable in that it involved rather less startling sink rates and enabled the crew to check undercarriage extension at an altitude where fuel consumption was still relatively modest. Basically, this took the form of an en route penetration in clean configuration to 20,000 ft (6096 m), the rate of descent rising from 2,000 to 6,000 ft/min (610–1829 m) as the aircraft neared the 20,000 ft (6096 m) mark. Once there, the undercarriage was lowered and a constant 4,000 ft/min (1219 m) rate was maintained for the rest of the way down, the entire descent taking some 11 minutes.

Regardless of which type of let-down procedure was employed, it was still necessary to carry the flight through to a logical conclusion, namely a safe approach and landing. As already noted, during the Stratojet's first three years of service this was certainly the most dangerous moment and there is no doubt that the unusual undercarriage configuration caused problems from time to time. Other factors which almost certainly contributed to some landing accidents were that the basic airframe was very 'clean' and therefore often reluctant to stop flying whilst the landing speed was relatively high, exceeding that of the later B-52 which of course also benefitted from the fitment of more responsive J57 engines and wing spoilers.

The fact that the J47 engines took time to spool up—somewhere between 12 and 20 seconds to go from idle to full power—combined with the remarkably clean airframe to make landing the B-47 a quite demanding exercise, it being necessary to achieve a reasonable compromise between maintaining sufficient power to ensure that an overshoot was possible whilst at the same time not coming in too 'hot' and facing the risk of overrunning.

Other factors also played no small part in flying a good approach and landing. For instance, it was imperative to avoid the danger of inducing a stall

Seemingly hanging motionless, B-47B 12263 receives a 'drink' from a KC-97F, such contacts being accomplished with increasing regularity as SAC's bomber and tanker assets increased in the early 1950s. By the middle of that decade, the KC-97 was 'hooking-up' somewhere in the world at intervals of no more than three and a half minutes (Boeing via Michael O'Leary)

which in turn meant that it was desirable to establish the final approach at the earliest possible moment to limit the amount of manoeuvring when the margin for error was small.

At a typical landing weight of 100,000-lb (45,359 kg), the most desirable approach speed was 128 knots (237 km/h), this being some 14 knots (26 km/h) above the stall speed when flying straight and level and assuming the absence of turbulence or wind shear near the threshold. Approach procedures naturally varied according to requirements of local ATC, terrain, etc.

At US bases pattern flying was routine, the downwind leg being flown at an altitude of 1,500 ft (457 m) at best approach speed plus 30 knots (ie about 158 knots). Turn on to the base leg occurred about 45 seconds after passing the end of the active runway and, whilst turning, the excess speed was bled off so that if the turn was executed precisely the Stratojet would roll-out on to final approach at about the 128-knot mark, having simultaneously descended to 800 ft (244 m).

Since the B-47 was designed to land, taxi and takeoff in the same attitude, power management was always critical. It was usual to maintain a setting of about 55 per cent until it was clear that the landing could be accomplished safely and the aircraft brought to a halt without careering off the end of the runway in the general direction of the next county. As far as the actual touch-down was concerned, this, too, was a critical moment for one could easily get into difficulties.

Ideally, both sets of main gear should have made contact with the runway simultaneously although, in practice, this seems to have been quite a rare occurrence. If the aft unit touched first, the landing could usually be completed quite safely since the aircraft usually settled down quite happily as speed diminished following deployment of the 32-ft (10-m) diameter braking parachute. Conversely, if the forward unit touched first on a 'hot' landing, trouble often ensued and the fact that the twin parachutes tended to hold the aircraft in a slightly tail-high attitude didn't exactly help.

Basically, a phenomenon known as 'weathercocking' or 'porpoising' often followed, sometimes with

Seen taxying in at Castle AFB, California, in June 1956, B-47E 2169 was in fact built by Douglas at Tulsa, Oklahoma, and may have been operating with the 93rd Bomb Wing at the time. The 93rd, of course, only utilized B-47s for just over a year, progressing to the Stratojet's rather larger stablemate, the massive B-52, in a transition programme which began in the summer of 1955 (USAF via Paul Bennett)

spectacular and, all too often, fatal results. Essentially, porpoising referred to a tendency for the aircraft to bounce back into the air in a nose-high attitude, and when this happened it was vital to get back into the correct landing attitude pretty damn quick or one could very soon 'buy the farm'—to employ contemporary vernacular. Power management played an important part in avoiding the worst consequences for if one had sufficient thrust available one could initiate an overshoot and try again. If, however, the rpm setting had been reduced to idle, the slow response time would preclude recovery by use of the throttles and, indeed, could well make matters worse, for the extra thrust would not become available until the aircraft had bounced a second time. Even then, it was not unknown for power to come up unevenly and the resulting asymmetric thrust often caused a wing to drop. In such situations, the amount of aileron available was often insufficient to stop the wing from striking the ground, an event which usually closely presaged a cartwheel and a big bang.

This was by no means the only problem to be faced when landing, but if one played it fairly close to the book the Stratojet was no more hazardous than any other aircraft and in certain circumstances, such as cross-wind landings, it was probably safer.

Needless to say, though, 'Murphy's Law' was most definitely applicable and probably claimed quite a few victims over the years, a classic instance of this relating to the rather novel approach parachute which was added to the B-47 at an early stage to enhance glide path control and so make landing safer and 'easier'. Almost inevitably, 'Murphy's Law' decreed that there were quite a few occasions when the pilot pulled the wrong lever and released the rather larger braking parachute instead. Such occurrences probably induced a few heart-stopping moments while the pilot wondered what on earth was happening when the airspeed and altitude needles went haywire as the aircraft decelerated and descended dramatically.

In case all of the foregoing tends to convey the impression that the Stratojet was viewed as being a bit of a 'dog', let me hasten to add that this would, by and large, be an erroneous conclusion. Obviously, there were those who viewed it with suspicion and hostility but there were many more who had nothing but praise for the B-47, looking back on their association with it with affection.

It undoubtedly had its vices and there were clearly a number of hazards awaiting those who thought they could bend the rules. If one was cognisant of the laws

LEFT
With the braking parachute fully deployed and with smoke pouring from the main wheels, the fifth B-47A returns to Wichita Air Force Base (later McConnell) at the end of a training sortie. The prominent badge on the nose of this aircraft signifies assignment to the Crew Training Air Force at Wichita, a unit which later used a large number of TB-47Bs
(via Robert F Dorr)

The second MacDill-based unit to receive the Stratojet was the 305th Bomb Wing which transitioned from the B-29 in 1952. One of the last units to acquire the initial major production model, the 305th was largely equipped with aircraft from the B-47B-50-BW block, such as 12323 seen here staging through Loring AFB at the start of a 90-day period of overseas rotational training. Basic finish is typical of the early period of Stratojet service, one particularly noteworthy feature being the deactivation of the integral RATO system, the ports for the nine bottles being covered over with a new piece of skin. Also worthy of mention is the badge on the nose section, this being that of the 364th Bomb Squadron. Although wing badges were regularly carried by B-47s, individual squadron insignia was seldom displayed in this fashion and, indeed, the 305th BW may well have been unique in adopting this policy (USAF via Robert F Dorr)

of gravity and aerodynamics and was fully conversant with and, perhaps more important, observant of the various manuals, it was unlikely that one would fall in harm's way. If, however, one was inclined to ignore such considerations, one only did so at one's peril for the Stratojet was not exactly forgiving. As I said right at the start of this chapter, it was never a type that suffered fools gladly. . .

Chapter 7
Operational Service — The Early Years

Although SAC had gained a fair amount of experience in the operation of jet aircraft by the autumn of 1951, it should be emphasized that such activities were predominantly concerned with the long-range fighter escort mission, a role which, while significant, was probably of little value in preparing the Command for the era of the jet bomber, an era which was ushered in shortly before the end of that same year.

However, in addition to the fighter role, a modest amount of expertize had also been gained with the North American RB-45 Tornado, this four-engined reconnaissance aircraft having entered service with the 91st Strategic Reconnaissance Group at Barksdale AFB, Louisiana during the summer of 1950. Although destined to serve with SAC for little more than three years, the RB-45 was rather more relevant in that it provided a foretaste of the logistical and other problems inherent in operating large jet aircraft whilst also helping to pave the way for the mass transatlantic and transpacific flights which later became such a routine and commonplace feature of SAC operations.

Indeed, the RB-45C hit the headlines on 29 July 1952 when a single example piloted by Major Louis H Carrington of the 91st Strategic Reconnaissance Wing successfully accomplished the first non-stop transpacific flight. Kicking-off from Elmendorf AFB in Alaska, the Tornado landed safely at Yokota AB, Japan, an achievement which earned Carrington and his fellow crew members the prestigious Mackay Trophy.

Not surprisingly, in-flight air refuelling support was an essential feature of this award-winning flight, the RB-45C receiving fuel from two KB-29s whilst, just a couple of weeks earlier, aerial refuelling by KB-29 had also played a vital part in the deployment of nearly 60 F-84G Thunderjets of the 31st Fighter-Escort Wing from Turner AFB, Georgia, to Misawa

and Chitose ABs in Japan, the epic 10,919-mile (17,572-km) journey being successfully accomplished in 10 days. Three months later, the 27th FEW surpassed that achievement when it moved 75 F-84Gs some 8,000-miles (12,875 km) from Bergstrom AFB, Texas, to Misawa although bad weather interrupted the transit which eventually took 11 days to complete. Nevertheless, early deployments such as these proved that in-flight refuelling had at last attained maturity, rather fortuitously at a most opportune moment for, since the B-47's range was modest when compared with the massive Convair B-36 and the forthcoming Boeing B-52, it can be readily comprehended that such support would be essential in implementing SAC's war plans in the event of conflict.

As far as SAC was concerned, the jet bomber era finally opened in earnest on 23 October 1951 when the first example of a production-standard B-47B (serial number 50-008) was formally handed over at Boeing's facility in Wichita, Kansas. Receiving the Stratojet on behalf of SAC, the Commanding Officer of the 306th Bombardment Wing, Colonel Michael 'Mike' McCoy, wasted little time in ferrying this

One of the first bases to receive the Stratojet, both of March's wings had converted to the B-47E model when this study was taken in the mid-1950s. Command insignia and the star-spangled sash are typical for the B-47—less typical is the presence of two stars on a dark background on the fuselage side, but this may well have indicated that the aircraft concerned carried the name of the Commanding General of the locally based 15th Air Force (Boeing)

Night scene at March. Diagonal lines on the fins of these B-47Bs indicate assignment to the 320th Bomb Wing at this California base. The second airfield to host Stratojet-equipped units, March's first resident wing was the 22nd BW which began receiving the B-47 in 1952 (USAF via Paul Bennett)

LEFT
Stable mates from the Boeing line share hangar accommodation, the nose section of a KC-97F Stratofreighter dominating the foreground while a pristine B-47B can be seen behind. Unusually, the Stratojet lacks command insignia, this possibly indicating that it had just returned from extensive post-production modification (Joe Bruch via Paul Bennett)

aircraft to its designated operational base, flying from Wichita to MacDill on the same day.

This delivery flight effectively marked the start of the 306th's transition from the B-29 and B-50 to the B-47 and also represented the culmination of an extensive and expensive period of preparation, which included the construction of a new 10,000 ft (3048 m) runway and fuel farm specifically to support B-47 operations, specialized training in the intricacies of the jet engine for the 306th BW's mechanics, high-speed navigation training for those more used to the sedate and lumbering B-29s and a modest amount of jet tuition in the Lockheed T-33A for those pilots earmarked to fly SAC's latest acquisition.

Seemingly, all that could be done had been done to prepare for the great moment, but it is probably fair to say that there was a certain amount of trepidation

amongst those who waited at MacDill to officially welcome Colonel McCoy at the end of his flight from Wichita and, certainly, there must have been many for whom this day would provide a first opportunity to study the Stratojet 'in the flesh'.

It was one of the latter who succeeded in reducing what should have been a well-ordered event into something approaching farce, although with the benefit of hindsight his over-zealous reaction was excusable, albeit highly embarrassing. As the B-47B swept in for its landing, the characteristic black exhaust trail left by the six J47 jet engines hung like smoke in the warm Florida air, prompting an alert and observant fire chief to reach the false conclusion that the new arrival was on fire and leading him to order his fleet of fire trucks into rapid action with the result that a bemused Colonel McCoy was halted on the runway and left to watch helplessly as fire retarding foam was directed into each of the brand new J47 engines. Regretfully, history does not record Colonel McCoy's comments on this unfortunate mishap whilst the fate of the fire chief concerned must remain a matter of conjecture, although, in the circumstances, it is doubtful if he was commended for his prompt response and display of initiative.

Just under a month later, on 19 November, B-47B 50-008 was officially christened *The Real McCoy* at MacDill and by year-end it had been joined by about a dozen more B-47Bs as the 306th BW became more heavily embroiled in the lengthy process of transition from piston to jet propulsion, these being the forerunners of a fleet which, by 1956–57, had multiplied enormously to a peak of more than 1,500 aircraft.

As if the task of transition was not enough, the 306th BW was also employed in a pioneering role, being entrusted with the vital job of formulating and evaluating combat concepts and techniques, a duty which essentially entailed writing the manuals for succeeding units. Consequently, it was hardly surprising that the 306th took some considerable time to regain full operational status and, indeed, it was not until the summer of 1953 that it was considered ready to go overseas for a 90-day rotational training deployment.

In the meantime, Exercise Sky Try—conducted between 22 January and 20 February 1953—verified that the B-47 was at last close to being adjudged combat ready, this exhaustive (and, as far as the 306th was concerned, exhausting) exercise successfully evaluating all aspects of the Stratojet under highly realistic simulated combat conditions.

By then, of course, a number of other units—most notably the 305th Bomb Wing, also at MacDill, and the 22nd Bomb Wing at March AFB, California— were also engaged in converting to Boeing's still relatively new bomber and it might be instructive to digress here for a while in order to study the growth of SAC's B-47 force before examining the deployment methods employed by the Command at the time the Stratojet made its debut.

As with any new type of combat aircraft, the early period of Stratojet operations was marked by cautious expansion and, indeed, by the end of 1952, more than a year after the first had been delivered, only just over 60 B-47Bs had entered the inventory. Most of these had been assigned to the 306th BW whilst a modest number had joined the 305th BW which, by design, was also located at MacDill. Preparations to equip a third wing, namely the 22nd at March, were undoubtedly far advanced although it appears that this had to wait until early 1953 to receive its first example of the B-47.

That same year was one of considerable expansion,

Spewing out the characteristic cloud of black smoke, a B-47B begins its departure roll while four more aircraft move into position for a minimum-interval takeoff (MITO), this being just one way of ensuring the survival of a substantial portion of SAC's bomber assets in the event of a surprise attack
(Boeing via Paul Bennett)

BELOW
Streaming its braking parachute, B-47B-50-BW 12318 of the 365th Bomb Squadron, 305th Bomb Wing, completes the flight from MacDill at the start of a wing-sized rotation. Loring AFB in Maine was the most commonly-used staging-point for deployments to British SAC bases between 1953 and 1956 when 'Reflex Action' signalled an end to the mass movement of bombers. Such deployments typically involved an overnight stop in Maine before proceeding across the Atlantic Ocean
(USAF via Robert F Dorr)

OVERLEAF
Virtually the entire complement of the 306th Air Refuelling Squadron may be seen in this view of the MacDill flight line. Taking delivery of its first KC-97E in July 1951, the 306th ARS spearheaded a huge tanker fleet, no less than 36 squadrons eventually operating the Stratofreighter by the mid-1950s when SAC's Stratojet fleet was also at its peak.
(USAF via David Ostrowski)

five additional units turning in their vintage B-29 'Superforts' for Boeing's jet-powered successor and by December the number on charge had grown substantially, having moved handsomely into three figures and surpassed the 300 mark by a fair margin. March AFB now hosted its second unit in the shape of the 320th BW whilst Lake Charles AFB, Louisiana had become the third 'dual-wing' base, being home to both the 44th and 68th BWs. The other two units which received the Stratojet in 1953 were the 301st BW at Barksdale and the 303rd BW at Davis-Monthan, both of these stations being new to the B-47 which was still very much in the process of finding its feet.

If the previous three years had been a period of cautious consolidation, the same claim certainly cannot be made of 1954 when Stratojet-equipped Bomb Wings seemed to be springing up all over the place, no less than 12 taking delivery of the B-47 during the course of the year. Davis-Monthan and Barksdale joined the ranks of the dual-wing bases by adding the 43rd and 376th BWs, these having previously been equipped with the B-50 and B-29 respectively whilst other dual-wing bases which stood up were Hunter (2nd and 308th BWs, ex-B-50 and B-29 respectively), Pinecastle (19th and 321st BWs, ex-B-29 and 'new' respectively) and Smoky Hill (40th and 310th BWs, both ex B-29). Further wings which converted to the B-47 were the 9th at Mountain Home (ex B-29), the 93rd at Castle (ex B-50), the 98th at Lincoln (ex B-29) and the 340th at Sedalia ('new'), this mass of additional units being in part responsible for the B-47 fleet rising to just under the 800-mark by December 1954.

Such a hectic rate of growth could hardly be sustained for any great length of time and, although the number of B-47s on hand surpassed the 1,000 mark in 1955, only five additional Bomb Wings picked up the Stratojet, these comprising the 96th at Altus, the 97th at Biggs, the 307th at Lincoln, the 380th at Plattsburgh and the 509th at Roswell. As far as previous equipment was concerned, the 307th had last used the B-29 but had been without aircraft following its return from combat duty in the Far East whilst both the 97th and the 509th traded in the B-50D, the former claiming the distinction of being the last unit to employ this type operationally in the pure bomber role. As far as the 96th and 380th BWs were concerned, these were both 'new' units, having been resurrected specifically to operate the B-47 and the same was true of the four Bomb Wings which acquired Boeing's medium jet bomber in 1956, these, for the record, being the 100th at Portsmouth, the 341st at Abilene, the 379th at Homestead and the 384th at Little Rock.

By December 1956, with the re-equipment process virtually at an end, SAC now featured no less than 1,306 B-47s in its operational inventory. More significantly, production of the B-47E was winding down but it was not until February 1957 that the re-equipment programme was formally considered to be complete when the 100th BW had received its full complement of 45 aircraft. Remarkably, one Wing—the 93rd at Castle—had already disposed of its Stratojets by this time although it should be pointed out that this unit employed the type primarily as a means of acquiring jet experience so as to smooth the upcoming hurdle of being the first SAC Wing to receive the massive B-52. Consequently, it never deployed operationally with the B-47.

Mention has already been made that the 305th and 22nd Bomb Wings were amongst the earliest units to receive the new bomber. To be precise, they were respectively the second and third units to convert to the Stratojet and they played no small part in enabling Boeing's bomber to attain full front-line status. Nevertheless, it was the 306th which continued to pave the way, another noteworthy instance of this unit's pioneering efforts coming in June when it faced the hurdle of its graduation exercise, this involving en masse overseas deployment by all three B-47 squadrons as well as the 20 KC-97Es of the associated 306th ARS.

Such deployments were, of course, now a regular feature of SAC, whose B-29s and B-50s had been visiting bases in the United Kingdom on rotational training missions since as early as 1948, this being a valuable adjunct to the Command's primary role of deterrence and one which greatly compounded Soviet targeting problems. In addition, of course, it also provided SAC elements with excellent training opportunities whilst simultaneously reducing retaliatory time in the event of conflict.

Hard to discern on the star-spangled sash, the small badge on the nose of this Douglas-built B-47E-10-DT identifies it as being assigned to the 380th Bomb Wing which operated Stratojets from Plattsburgh AFB, New York, from the summer of 1955 until December 1965. Still active today with the FB-111A, the 380th was one of two so-called 'super-strength' wings, operating no fewer than 70 Stratojets and 40 KC-97 Stratofreighters between July 1959 and June 1960
(via Robert F Dorr)

BELOW
Liberally coated with notices applied by various elements of the Wichita workforce, the 1,000th Stratojet to be built at the Kansas factory emerges from the assembly hall for the first time on 14 October 1954. Interest in this event was obviously great, judging from the number of people visible in this picture
(Boeing via Michael O'Leary)

The 306th's tour was, however, most significant in that it was the first wing-sized deployment to be made by a jet bomber unit and a considerable amount of ground-work had to be done in preparing for the graduation exercise, this extending to a preliminary visit to Fairford by Colonel McCoy in early April in order to check out the facilities at the designated deployment base. As far as is known, this was the very first overseas visit to be made by the B-47.

Staging initially from MacDill to Limestone AFB, Maine—in the process pioneering a route which was to be used by countless Stratojets in later years—McCoy's B-47 completed the 3,120-mile (5021 km) transatlantic sector in 5 hours 38 minutes, setting a new, but soon to be broken, record. However, the trip across was not entirely trouble-free, for, although due to land at Fairford, McCoy actually flew into Brize Norton following problems and discomfort arising from the pressure suits then worn by B-47 crew members. Eventually withdrawn from use on the grounds of being dangerous, the difficulties experienced with the suits by McCoy and his colleagues culminated in a decision to make an emergency landing at nearby Brize Norton which had better emergency services available, the Wing Commander eventually completing his journey to Fairford by road.

In the event, McCoy's preliminary inspection tour proved well advised, facilities at Fairford being found to be less than satisfactory which prompted a return visit by about 50 306th BW personnel in early May in order to bring the base up to the desired standard, a task which kept them more or less fully occupied for the next 30 days.

With all of the necessary preparatory work completed, the 306th BW eventually began to deploy from MacDill on 3 June, successive squadron-sized waves of 15 B-47Bs departing on that and the ensuing two days and following the same route taken by the Wing Commander in April. Each wave stopped overnight at Limestone (now Loring) before proceeding to Fairford where the 45 Stratojets all recovered safely between the 4th and 6th of June, McCoy's record being broken on no less than nine occasions over the three-day period, the best time of 5 hours 22 minutes being logged by the very last aircraft to reach the UK base. Although tanker support was not required during the deployment phase, the 306th ARS's fleet of 20 KC-97Es also flew simultaneously to England with support troops and equipment, these using a slightly different route and landing at a different airfield, proceeding via Harmon Air Base, Newfoundland to Mildenhall in Suffolk.

Remaining at Fairford for some three months, the 306th BW was kept fairly busy whilst overseas and accumulated a substantial amount of operational experience, flying simulated attack missions against a variety of targets in both the United Kingdom and Europe. In early September, with their 90-day tour complete, the 306th BW duly returned home although on this occasion the transatlantic trip was made non-stop from Fairford to MacDill, the redeploying Stratojets taking on fuel from 306th ARS KC-97s shortly after leaving England. As they

B-47E Stratojet 32334 had almost certainly been brought to a late modification status when it formed the subject of a sequence of 'round-the-clock' photographs that were taken at Wichita in the late 1950s. This retrospective work probably also included some structural strengthening as part of Project Milk Bottle which provided many B-47s with a new lease of life
(Boeing via Paul Bennett)

BELOW
Framed by the wing of a Stratojet, this portion of the ramp at March AFB, California, was normally occupied by the B-47s of the 320th Bomb Wing. One of a number of 'dual-wing' bases, March was also host to the 22nd BW and would have been home to no fewer than 90 Stratojets when both units were in residence
(Joe Bruch via Paul Bennett)

RIGHT
Possibly portrayed against a backdrop of the Sierra Nevada mountain range in California, B-47E-65-BW 17025 features typical late-service markings and inscriptions, the single coloured fin stripe perhaps indicating assignment to the 22nd Bomb Wing at March AFB. For a time in the latter half of the 1950s, this unit is known to have operated quite a few aircraft from this and adjacent production blocks
(via Robert F Dorr)

BOTTOM RIGHT
Production of the standard B-47E variant by the parent company terminated with 36244, a 'dash 135 aircraft which was handed over to Strategic Air Command in 1956. After an operational career of less than ten years, this particular machine was eventually preserved at Wright-Patterson AFB, Ohio, as part of the USAF Museum collection. This fine photograph was probably taken at around the time it was delivered to SAC, the variations in skin tone being particularly evident in the vicinity of the rear fuselage
(via Robert F Dorr)

BELOW
SAC's star-studded sash and the badge of the 22nd Bomb Wing adorn the nose of this B-47E at March AFB in the latter half of the 1950s while another similarly marked Stratojet can be seen in the distance
(Joe Bruch via Paul Bennett)

departed, their place in the UK was filled by the B-47s of the 305th Bomb Wing which took up temporary residence at Brize Norton, whilst the 305th ARS KC-97 tankers went to Mildenhall. Once again, the tour of duty lasted for some three months and culminated in relief by the 22nd Bomb Wing which went to Upper Heyford in December.

The fourth British base to support B-47 rotational operations was Greenham Common which welcomed the 303rd Bomb Wing from Davis-Monthan AFB, Arizona, in March 1954 although their tenure was brief, problems experienced with the structural integrity of the runway and hard standings necessitating a move to Fairford in April for the remainder of the 90-day tour. One other British airfield also hosted B-47 units during the rotational training era, this being Lakenheath which was first visited by the 321st Bomb Wing from Pinecastle AFB, Florida, in December 1954.

TOP
Resplendent in pristine factory-fresh condition, the second example of the RB-47E is seen during the course of a pre-delivery test flight from Wichita, Kansas. Production of this variant eventually terminated when 240 had been completed for service with five Strategic Reconnaissance Wings, a further 15 machines being turned out by Boeing as B-47Ks. In the event, the RB-47E enjoyed only a modestly successful career, the phase-out process beginning in October 1957, little more than two years after the last aircraft was delivered
(USAF via Robert F Dorr)

MIDDLE
Lack of gun armament, sealed-over RATO ports, the large 'last two' of the serial number and the badge on the forward fuselage all help to identify this Stratojet as a TB-47B. Most of the 60-odd TB-47Bs were stationed at McConnell AFB, Kansas (formerly Wichita AFB) as part of Air Training Command's Crew Training Air Force (Crew TAF) which was responsible for all B-47 tuition and which later became the 3520th Combat Crew Training Wing. Eventually, in July 1958, SAC took control, simultaneously establishing the 4347th CCTW at the same base
(USAF via Robert F Dorr)

BOTTOM
A quartet of 320th Bomb Wing B-47B-IIs bask in late afternoon sunshine at March AFB, California, rather coincidentally in March 1956. At that time, this base was home for more than 90 Stratojets and 40 KC-97 Stratofreighters
(Joe Bruch via Paul Bennett)

Whilst in England, command jurisdiction and operational control of SAC units engaged in rotational training duty was entrusted to the 7th Air Division which had been established at South Ruislip on 20 March 1951 and which subsequently moved to new quarters at High Wycombe in the early sixties. Between June 1953 and April 1958 when the method of rotation changed significantly, this organisation was to temporarily exercise control over no less than 20 B-47-equipped Wings, three of which (the 40th, 68th and 310th BWs) made two visits. During the same period, at least one fully-fledged B-47 Bomb Wing was in temporary residence at any given time whilst there were brief interludes in 1954 and 1955 when two Wings were present at different airfields.

Incidentally, although most deployments were of 90-day duration, it was not unknown for shorter periods to be spent overseas, SAC units being called upon to undertake 30, 45 and 60-day tours from time to time, an example being provided by the 68th Bomb Wing which was present at Fairford for just under 50 days between May and July 1955.

A rather less widely publicized but no less significant aspect of the 7th Air Division's mission was that of maintaining the UK air bases in a state of readiness to support SAC's war plans, for, in common with other facilities in Morocco and, later, Spain, these would have played a key role had the Command been called upon to commit its forces to action and implement the EWO (emergency war order).

The advent of the B-47 in really substantial numbers more or less coincided with a significant and radical change in SAC's concept of force employment. Prior to 1954, the Command anticipated despatching bomber aircraft to forward bases where they would be fuelled and armed before departing to attack their targets. By the summer of 1954, however, it was becoming apparent that this policy was somewhat laborious and, in certain circumstances, likely to be potentially injurious to SAC's retaliatory capability since there was no longer any guarantee that the foreign bases would survive long enough to permit their use by transient bombers.

Accordingly, a new method was conceived whereby aircraft would depart from the USA, perform their bombing mission and then recover at an overseas base, taking advantage of in-flight refuelling support if necessary. This concept was successfully evaluated by the 38th Air Division at Hunter AFB, Georgia during the summer of 1954 when the two Bomb Wings assigned to this organization—the 2nd and the 308th—participated in Operation Leap Frog in which a number of B-47s left their Georgia base and flew a simulated bombing mission before landing at Sidi Slimane, Morocco, this being the first of many similar exercises to be conducted during the mid-to-late-fifties.

As far as the 7th AD in England was concerned, it is obvious that forces already in situ would have been

committed to action in the event of war but the airfields from which they would have operated were also designated as post-strike recovery bases and this aspect of operations was exhaustively evaluated on a number of occasions. Such 'Post-Strike' exercises varied considerably in scope but this period of SAC's history witnessed many instances of B-47s and B-36s undertaking simulated combat missions involving departure from their US bases, followed by transatlantic flights which culminated in 'attacks' against 'targets' such as Rome, Paris, and London.

On completion of these 'strikes', some of the bombers involved would recover at the English bases whilst others went to North Africa. Here, they would remain for a few days before returning home, no doubt engaging in post-strike de-briefing and generally assessing their performance. In addition to Operation Leap Frog, which proved the validity of the concept, Exercise Open Mind, conducted in February 1955, culminated in B-47s of the 22nd, 301st, 303rd and 376th Bomb Wings recovering in England whilst, two months later, Fairford was invaded by more than 60 Arizona-based Stratojets when the 43rd and 303rd Bomb Wings took part in 'Boiler Maker' and there were undoubtedly many more similar missions.

As already noted, England was by no means the only overseas country which supported SAC bombers engaged in rotational training exercises, but it was certainly the first. As the decade progressed, however, the B-47 became a familiar sight in other skies as it flexed its wings. Morocco was next to host B-47s although, once again, it should be borne in mind that SAC units had been visiting this country for some considerable time, the 5th Air Division having moved from Offutt AFB, Nebraska, to Rabat as early as mid-June 1951, initially to supervise construction of the massive air bases at Sidi Slimane, Ben Guerir and Nouasseur and subsequently to exercise command jurisdiction over elements assigned there on a temporary duty (TDY) basis. Consequently, examples of the B-29, B-36 and B-50 had all been despatched to Morocco at various times between 1951 and February 1954 when the first Wing-sized visit was made by the B-47, Barksdale's 301st Bomb Wing being the unit concerned and Sidi Slimane the host base. Subsequently, Ben Guerir also accommodated B-47 Wings from January 1955

Wall-to-wall airplanes! Close to 50 Stratojets from the 22nd and 320th Bomb Wings occupy the vast concrete expanse of March AFB's main hard-standing area in a scene which was typical of the spring of 1956. On the aircraft in the foreground, the anti-flash curtain has been drawn, presumably to keep the cockpit temperature from rising to unbearable levels
(Joe Bruch via Paul Bennett)

onwards, the first unit to undergo TDY at this facility being the 306th which, evidently, was still conducting its pioneering activities. The third major installation in Morocco—Nouasseur AB—evidently did not welcome B-47s at this time although it did play host to a couple of B-36 Wings during 1955 and ultimately supported 'Reflex Action' in later years.

On the other side of the world, in the Far East, the B-47 also became a fairly familiar sight, although, with suitable air bases being relatively few and far between and with a more limited range of target options, it was not assigned to that theatre in anything like the numbers seen in North Africa and Europe. The Stratojet's first visit to the Far East was made as early as June 1954 when a trio of 22nd Bomb Wing aircraft flew non-stop from March AFB, California, to Yokota AB in Japan, in the process establishing a record for the longest non-stop point-to-point flight made by the Stratojet by covering the 6,700-miles

(10,782-km) in less than 15 hours with two refuellings en route.

Unlike England, however, this visit did not herald regular deployments and, indeed, the standard B-47 was never destined to operate from Japan in any significant quantities although RB-47s of the 55th SRW later became a most familiar sight and sound at Yokota. In point of fact, apart from a brief Wing-sized deployment made to Kadena, Okinawa by the 9th BW in October 1955, bomber versions of the Stratojet operated only from Andersen AFB, Guam, under the control of the 3rd Air Division which had been established there on 18 June 1954 and which, between mid-October 1954 and early July 1956, hosted a succession of B-36 Bomb Wings, this type eventually being supplanted by the B-47 when the 303rd BW took up temporary residence on 4 July.

During the next two years, Andersen was permanently occupied by Stratojets, six other Bomb Wings spending 90-day periods there before the 303rd returned on 5 April 1958 for its second visit. When the 303rd eventually re-deployed to Davis-Monthan on 4 July 1958, it brought a significant chapter in SAC history to a close for this was the very last 90-day TDY to be made by any SAC Wing. Thereafter, 'Reflex Action' and 'Air Mail' formed the basis by which the pure bomber versions of the Stratojet were deployed at overseas bases.

Featuring old-style small service inscriptions in concert with white anti-flash undersides, B-47E 2352 was one of 386 aircraft produced by Lockheed at Marietta in Georgia and was almost certainly assigned to either the 305th or 306th Bomb Wing when this photograph was taken in the mid-1950s
(USAF via Robert F Dorr)

Chapter 8
Decline and Fall

It is probably fair to say that 1957 was the high-water mark as far as B-47 operations were concerned. Certainly, SAC's re-equipment programme was completed in February of that year, the 100th Bomb Wing at Pease being the last unit to receive its full complement of aircraft, this bringing the total number of active Wings to 28, each of which was nominally equipped with 45 B-47s distributed equally between three squadrons. In reality, however, each Wing probably had about 50 Stratojets on hand.

At the start of the year SAC still subscribed heavily towards the rotational training policy by which complete Wings deployed overseas for periods of temporary duty which could last up to three months. However, big changes were looming, these affecting methods of operation both at home and overseas and, as usual, SAC moved cautiously, conducting a number of exhaustive evaluations and tests as part of the process of proving the major conceptual changes which were then in prospect.

The first—and, almost certainly, the most significant—of these ultimately affected all US-based bomber units since it entailed adoption of the so-called 'one-third alert'. Essentially, this called for all SAC units to maintain approximately one-third of their bomber and tanker resources on ground alert and, as far as the bombers were concerned, in a fully-armed state, ready for immediate take-off should the need arise.

Prompted mainly by the threat posed by ever more reliable Soviet ICBMs (intercontinental ballistic missiles) which, in theory at least, could conceivably knock-out major US bases before any retaliatory forces could get airborne, the alert programme was quite clearly one of the most far-reaching manifestations of the ever-evolving theory of deterrence to be implemented during the course of the fifties.

Nevertheless, despite perceiving a need for urgency, SAC resisted the pressure to move prematurely, instead conducting three major field tests in order to satisfy itself and other elements of the defence hierarchy that such a method of operation was indeed feasible, whilst simultaneously pinpointing those areas of organisation and administration which would need to be changed before alert duty could be introduced on a fleet-wide basis. With its usual penchant for allocating code names, the three tests were all given formal titles by SAC although these were by no means so bizarre as some and, indeed, they even appeared to have some relevance to the job in hand.

The first such trial—Operation Try Out—had in fact begun in November 1956 when the 38th Air Division's two Bomb Wings (2nd and 308th BWs) and two KC-97 tanker squadrons (2nd and 308th ARSs) endeavoured to maintain one-third of their assets in alert status at Hunter AFB, Georgia. In this, they were essentially successful although 'Try Out' did reveal that further refinement was necessary if the system was to be adopted on a wholesale basis by other elements of SAC.

Accordingly, SAC headquarters directed two more evaluations, the first of which was Operation Watch Tower, conducted by elements of the 825th Air Division (70th SRW, 384th BW and 70th ARS) from Little Rock AFB, Arkansas, between April and November 1957 whilst further detail changes were addressed by Operation Fresh Approach which was entrusted to the B-47s and KC-97s of the 9th BW at Mountain Home AFB, Idaho, during September 1957. Between them, these three studies proved that ground alert was indeed a practicable proposition and the Commander-in-Chief, General Thomas S Power, wasted little time in introducing this new concept, directing that such operations begin at a number of US and overseas air bases with effect from 1 October 1957, coincidentally just two weeks before

the first Stratojet was consigned to the 'boneyard' and little more than a month before the first Wing was inactivated.

Although ground alert was now a feature of SAC operations, it was still very much in its infancy and the early period was one of detailed study which eventually led to major changes in the organisation of Stratojet-equipped Bomb Wings. Operational experience gained during the opening months of 1958 soon revealed a need for administrative changes, the necessity to maintain a substantial amount of resources on alert duty adding a fourth aspect to SAC's normal day-to-day cyclical routine of one day spent on flight planning, one day spent flying and one day off duty.

Since operations now fell into a four-cycle pattern and since support elements were also affected, it was decided to reorganise most of the Combat Wings in a programme which formally got under way on 1

TOP
Based at Plattsburgh, New York, the 380th Bomb Wing operated the B-47 for almost exactly a decade, disposing of this type during the course of 1965. Prior to that, it had been redesignated as a Strategic Aerospace Wing on 15 September 1964, when it assumed control of an Atlas ICBM squadron. One of this wing's B-47Es, 0-32399, is seen on alert at a UK base (via Lindsay Peacock)

MIDDLE
Although the 55th SRW could justifiably lay claim to having been SAC's most unusual Stratojet-operating unit, the two Lockbourne-based Bomb Wings were what could certainly be described as 'odd-balls'. Both units—the 301st and 376th BWs—were equipped with the EB-47E for several years, these being distinguished by virtue of the bulged bomb bay area. This contained a removable sensor package featuring an array of ECM 'goodies' but very little has ever been said about this equipment although it appears that these EB-47Es would have been employed in a kind of 'escort' role, furnishing ECM support to pure bomber aircraft intent on penetrating Soviet territory in the event of nuclear war (Aviation Photo News)

BOTTOM
With the 30-bottle RATO installation, 380th Strategic Aerospace Wing B-47E 0-32110 idles away the hours on nuclear alert duty at Brize Norton in late September 1964. The white anti-flash undersides and natural metal upper surfaces were typical of the finish applied to SAC's dwindling fleet of Stratojets at this time (Paul Bennett)

September 1958 at Little Rock and Lincoln. Subsequently, with effect from October 1958, one base in each of the three numbered Air Forces (2nd, 8th and 15th) would be reorganized on the first day of the month.

As far as the B-47 Bomb Wings were concerned, reorganization involved adding an extra Bombardment Squadron and this eventually led to the activation of some 27 additional squadrons between 1 September 1958 and 1 May 1959, only the 97th BW not being affected since it disposed of the B-47 in January 1959, subsequently being re-equipped with the B-52G. Strategic Reconnaissance Wings, which did not stand nuclear alert duty, were not affected by the reorganization to quite the same degree.

With regard to the fate of the extra squadrons, some disappeared with their parent Wings during 1960–61 as the B-47 phase-out process accelerated whilst the others eventually fell victim to further reorganization, largely as a result of changes in alert posture introduced by SAC in response to President Kennedy's March 1961 directive that the Command maintain no less than 50 per cent of its bombers and tankers in 'cocked' status. Since this had a significant impact on unit organization and since the four-cycle pattern was greatly disrupted by the additional alert commitment, virtually all of the surviving extra squadrons ceased operations in October 1961 although it was not until 1 January 1962 that the 18 which remained in being were finally discontinued and inactivated.

At about the time of the 1958 reorganization, dispersal of SAC combat echelons also began to make headway although this had little immediate impact on the disposition of the B-47 fleet nor, unlike the B-52, did it result in wholesale changes of base. Rather, with phase-out of the Stratojet anticipated to begin in earnest in the not-too-distant future, SAC was content to wait and let the course of inactivation achieve the desired objective.

In addition to introducing revised methods of operation within the continental USA, SAC also greatly modified its philosophy with regard to overseas-based elements, ending the long-established rotational training deployment programme and adopting a far more flexible and responsive system in its place. Known by the code name 'Reflex Action', this system made its debut in North Africa during the summer of 1957 and remained a key feature of SAC policy until the last B-47Es were withdrawn from overseas bases during the spring of 1965.

As was the case with US-based bomber elements, one of the prime considerations in the adoption of 'Reflex Action' was that of enhancing deterrent posture and capability, this deployment mode being introduced at about the same time as the one-third alert programme made its debut in the USA. In practice, however, higher levels of combat readiness were achieved by elements undergoing 'Reflex

Action' and, although precise details of the number of bombers committed to 'Reflex'—and, incidentally, still are—classified, it is known that all of them were held on alert in a 'cocked' configuration, armed and ready to launch within 15 minutes of the order being given.

Since Reflex aircraft never flew when on alert, this operation was doubly beneficial in that not only did it result in a significant increase in potential attack effectiveness but it also permitted this to be achieved at reduced cost. Yet another benefit concerned airframe fatigue, the lower utilization levels extending the projected service lives of SAC's B-47s.

Initially introduced on an experimental basis in Morocco, physical preparation for Reflex Action began a few days before the end of June 1957 when four 2nd Air Force Bomb Wings—to be precise, the 2nd and 308th at Hunter plus the 305th and 306th at MacDill—each despatched five B-47s to Sidi Slimane Air Base. Thereafter, fresh aircraft and crews rotated periodically from the USA for brief periods of temporary duty at the Moroccan base whilst SAC continued to monitor the effectiveness of this method of operation and, more specifically, its likely impact on deterrent capability. Having satisfactorily established that Reflex represented a marked improvement over previous deployment policy, Headquarters SAC duly made plans to adopt the same system at other overseas bases as soon as was practicable whilst, in the meantime, a substantial portion of the 20 Reflex bombers at Sidi Slimane began to stand nuclear alert with effect from 1 October 1957, this essentially marking the start of an operation which was to last nearly eight years.

More widespread adoption of Reflex followed in early 1958, the new year being just seven days old when the British bases at Fairford and Greenham Common began to host B-47s assigned to this duty. At the beginning, elements assigned to these bases were drawn from different wings, Fairford receiving aircraft from the 2nd, 308th and 384th BWs whilst Greenham Common drew upon the 98th, 307th and 310th BWs for its Reflex echelon. Subsequently, following the completion of the 100th BW's 90-day tour at the beginning of April 1958, Brize Norton also converted to Reflex, B-47s of the 2nd and 308th BWs being consigned here.

'Reflex Action' forces of alert-dedicated B-47Es remained at both Brize Norton and Upper Heyford until the end of March 1965 when they finally stood down in anticipation of returning to the USA for the last time. This picture, taken at a rather misty Brize Norton on 21 March of that year, shows one of the last Stratojets to undergo alert duty. The aircraft concerned, 0-31884, was from the 380th SAW at Plattsburgh AFB, New York
(Paul Bennett)

In the following summer, the method of assigning aircraft changed quite radically, at least as far as British bases were concerned. Rather than have two or three Wings furnishing aircraft to a single base, it was decided to implement what might best be described as a 'Wing-Base' concept, in which one air base supported one Bomb Wing. Introduced on 1 July 1958, this resulted in further realignment and the same date also witnessed the addition of Mildenhall as a forward operating location for bombers assigned to Reflex Action duty, B-47s from the 310th BW henceforth fulfilling Reflex obligations from this base rather than Greenham Common as had previously been the case.

As far as Greenham Common was concerned, the 98th and 307th BW turned over alert responsibility to the 40th BW at the same time, while Fairford's remaining element—the 384th BW—also departed, to be relieved by the 68th BW. Over at nearby Brize Norton, the changeover appears to have been accomplished slightly differently, with the 308th BW disappearing from the scene at the end of June leaving only the 2nd BW in residence.

In fact, Brize Norton was perhaps slightly unusual in that, from the beginning of August, this also served as a temporary home for 301st BW aircraft. However, this unit was rather special since its primary task was that of electronic counter measures and its fleet of B-47Es were distinctly different from the standard bomber aircraft, being configured with a variety of ECM devices which would undoubtedly have been employed to disrupt Soviet defensive capability and thus improve the survivability of penetrating B-47s in the event of war. In simple terms, the task of the 301st BW could well be likened to that of 'riding shotgun' and it was a task which was later shared by the 376th BW which also resided at Lockbourne.

Further significant expansion in the size of the UK-based Reflex force occurred in early January 1959 when no less than three more bases began to host B-47s, these comprising Bruntingthorpe (100th BW), Chelveston (301st BW ECM aircraft) and Upper Heyford (98th BW) but as far as bases were concerned this represented a high-water mark and, indeed, three of them were duly transferred to the

The RB-47K variant was a particularly rare bird outside the confines of the continental USA, only 15 aircraft being built with Fiscal Year 1953 funding for service with just one squadron of the 55th Strategic Reconnaissance Wing at Forbes AFB, Kansas. Employed mainly on weather reconnaissance tasks, they are known to have performed daily flights over Alaska for several years, presumably to gather weather data relating to routes that would have been used by SAC bomber aircraft in the event of the emergency war order being promulgated (Boeing via Robert F Dorr)

TOP
The red stripe at the top of the fin of B-47E 0-17078 was
a common feature on aircraft of the 384th Bomb Wing
during 1963, when this unit was engaged in 'Reflex Action'
from RAF Greenham Common. This particular Stratojet
was one of a small number which 'reflexed' through the UK
with two different units in 1963, also visiting RAF
Fairford in Gloucestershire while assigned to the 340th
Bomb Wing
(John Hughes)

ABOVE
Also photographed at Greenham Common, B-47E 20597
was present for a while during the first quarter of 1964, by
which time the 384th BW's red fin stripe had apparently
been dropped. This Wing continued to furnish alert-
dedicated Stratojets to Greenham Common until the end of
March 1964
(John Hughes)

TOP

The 380th BW/SAW's association with Brize Norton was particularly long-lived, aircraft from this unit forming part of the 'Reflex' force at this Oxfordshire base for more than four years. One of the more interesting aircraft to be seen in 1963 was 0-32415 which carried the name City of Plattsburgh II *on the extreme nose section. Presentation of the 'last three' on the fin was another near-unique feature of the 380th's B-47Es*
(John Hughes)

ABOVE

A trio of 384th BW B-47Es on alert at Greenham Common in 1963. Home-based at Little Rock, Arkansas, the 384th first undertook 'Reflex Action' at Fairford between January and June 1958, returning to Greenham Common some five years later. Less than six months after returning to the USA, this wing was deactivated at the beginning of September 1964
(John Hughes)

control of the Third Air Force during the ensuing summer, simultaneously ceasing to support B-47 activities. First to go was Chelveston on 30 June, the 301st BW machines disappearing from the UK scene for almost a year whilst, at Bruntingthorpe, the newly-arrived 96th BW hardly had time to familiarize itself with its surroundings, aircraft from this Wing only being present from the 9th until the 23rd of July. The last base to lose its B-47s was Mildenhall and, once again, the unit involved—the 44th BW—enjoyed only brief tenure although in this instance it did at least remain in the UK, taking over from the 98th BW at Upper Heyford on 1 August. Thus, by the start of August 1959, the number of active SAC bases in the UK had fallen to just four, a level which was to be maintained for almost five years.

Other airfields which began supporting Reflex Action bomber forces during the 1957–58 timeframe included Moron, Torrejon and Zaragoza in Spain; Ben Guerir and Nouasseur in Morocco and Eielson and Elmendorf in Alaska whilst an essentially similar operation known by the code name 'Air Mail' was also introduced at Andersen AFB, Guam, with effect from about July 1958, the final 90-day TDY tour at that base being that made by the 303rd BW between early April and early July.

Essentially, Reflex Action was a method by which bomber forces could be stationed overseas in a heightened alert state for an indefinite period of time. Crews and aircraft engaged in Reflex Action were,

BOTTOM RIGHT
Present at Greenham Common during the 1962–63 time frame, aircraft of the 307th Bomb Wing normally featured a green stripe near the top of the fin and this was certainly carried by B-47E 31872 seen here moments before 'reflexing' back to home base at Lincoln, Nebraska (Aviation Photo News)

BELOW
Lockheed-built B-47E 31925 of the Pease, New Hampshire-based 100th Bomb Wing on 'Reflex Action' alert duty at RAF Brize Norton in the early 1960s. One of several units which 'reflexed' through this base, the 'Bloody Hundredth' was present from the summer of 1959 to the summer of 1960 and again from the summer of 1961 until the summer of 1962

however, in a near constant state of flux for individual tours of duty lasted just three weeks with the result that as one aircraft and crew returned home, another one arrived at the overseas location to take their place. In practice, changeover was normally accomplished over a two-day period, an arriving B-47 having to be prepared for nuclear alert duty before the Stratojet being relieved was permitted to stand down for redeployment to the USA. In this way, force size was maintained at a constant level.

As far as the aircraft were concerned, the entire 21-day tour was spent on alert status. The crews, however, followed a rather different pattern, this arising from the fact that there were always more crews available than aircraft. Thus, each 21-day spell of 'Reflex' duty began with a week on alert. This was followed by a week of rest and relaxation before returning to alert for the final week of the tour. Naturally, since there was a surplus of personnel, bomber crews did not always arrive or depart by B-47, many of them probably reaching their 'Reflex Action' station aboard the KC-97s and KC-135s which were fairly frequent visitors to most bases.

Thus, at any given time, all of the B-47s engaged in Reflex Action at any of the air bases which supported such forces, were kept on nuclear alert standby. On a global basis, this meant that a substantial amount of the B-47 fleet was always ready to go within 15 minutes of the order to launch being given by the National Command Authorities and some idea of the numbers involved can be gained from closer study of the situation in England during the first six months of 1963 when approximately 68 examples of the B-47E were present. No less than 20 of these were EB-47E ECM-configured aircraft from the 301st and 376th BWs at Lockbourne, the balance all being standard B-47E bombers.

By then, there had been some changes in the distribution of aircraft with the result that Greenham Common now hosted B-47Es from two units, the 96th SAW and the 307th BW sharing equally the responsibility for keeping a total of 18 here in temporary residence. Brize Norton and Upper Heyford also had Reflex forces drawn from two Wings. At Brize, the 301st BW and the 380th BW were to be found, these furnishing ten and nine aircraft respectively whilst Upper Heyford was occupied by the 98th and 376th BWs, the number of aircraft involved being nine and ten respectively. However, the Stratojets of the 301st and 376th BWs were, as noted elsewhere, EB-47Es assigned to ECM tasks and both were present throughout the year in question. The remaining base, at Fairford, was unique in that it supported aircraft from just one unit, this being the 340th BW with 12 examples of the B-47E normally in residence at any time.

The year of 1963 did, however, witness significant change in Reflex, at least as far as the UK bases were concerned. The first manifestation of this came in February when the 96th SAW ceased rotation at

Providing aircraft to two UK bases for a few months during 1964, the 380th Bomb Wing was a long time 'resident' at Brize Norton, where it maintained a permanent presence from autumn 1960 until the end of March 1965. B-47E 0-31947 was typical of the aircraft which could be seen here and at Upper Heyford in 1964 (Aviation Photo News)

Barbed wire entanglements surrounded the dispersal areas at RAF Brize Norton, where B-47E 0-32132 of the 380th SAW undergoes its three-week spell of alert duty in early 1965. Colours and markings were typical of aircraft of this wing (Paul Bennett)

Greenham Common, this subsequently disposing of the B-47 during March 1963. For the time being, the 307th BW continued to support Reflex from Greenham but major realignment of SAC's numbered Air Force structure at the beginning of July coincided with further changes in composition of the bomber forces engaged on temporary duty in the UK and the two events were almost certainly linked.

Another factor which almost certainly did have some bearing on force composition in the UK concerned the three Moroccan bases of Ben Guerir, Nouasseur and Sidi Slimane, all of which ceased to host Reflex B-47s in July. Certainly, with effect from 30 June, the 98th, 307th and 340th BWs stopped rotating to England, their places at Upper Heyford, Greenham Common, and Fairford being taken up on the following day by the 509th, 384th and 40th BWs respectively. This realignment also resulted in the number of aircraft engaged in Reflex being cut to 59, with the force now being organized as follows. At Fairford, the 40th BW kept nine B-47Es whilst Greenham housed 12 similar aircraft of the 384th BW. Brize Norton's complement remained unchanged at 19 and Upper Heyford also continued to accommodate 19, both of the latter two bases including ten EB-47Es amongst the aircraft present.

If the opening months of 1963 marked a high point, the following year can be said to have witnessed the beginning of the end as far as UK operations were concerned and yet no less than seven of the surviving 12 Stratojet-equipped Wings undertook Reflex Action duty in the UK at some time during 1964. Perhaps the most noteworthy early event was a quite complex realignment which saw the EB-47Es move from Brize Norton and Upper Heyford to Greenham Common and Fairford at the end of March. Thus, the Brize Norton-based EB-47Es of the 301st BW departed to Greenham Common, their place at Brize being filled by the standard B-47Es of the 40th SAW (redesignated from the 40th BW on 1 February) which came from Fairford. In turn, the latter base acquired the EB-47s of the 376th BW from Upper Heyford, their place being taken by B-47Es of the 380th BW. At Greenham Common, the previously resident unit— the 384th—departed to Little Rock where it disposed of the B-47E in the ensuing summer before being inactivated on 1 September. In addition, the 380th BW and 509th BW continued to provide B-47Es to Brize Norton and Upper Heyford respectively throughout 1964, the former unit being somewhat unusual in that it now also had aircraft at Upper Heyford as well.

In the event, the tenure of the EB-47Es at Fairford and Greenham Common proved to be rather brief for both the 301st and 376th BWs redeployed to Lockbourne at the end of May, their departure signalling the end of Reflex Action at these two airfields.

Brize Norton and Upper Heyford, however, were

RIGHT
On the verge of being swallowed up by the murk of a typical English winter's day, 384th Bomb Wing B-47E 20372 stands in 'cocked' configuration, ready to launch from Greenham Common within minutes of the alert being sounded
(via Robert F Dorr)

BELOW
One of the last units to employ the Stratojet as a pure bomber was the Lincoln, Nebraska-based 98th Strategic Aerospace Wing which eventually disposed of its B-47Es in December 1965 as part of the accelerated phase-out programme code-named 'Fast Fly'. Disposition of the B-47E fleet followed standard practice, most of the aircraft being flown to Davis-Monthan AFB, Arizona for storage and eventual scrapping and it was there, on the arrivals ramp, that B-47E 32154 was photographed on 2 November 1965
(Norman Taylor via Robert F Dorr)

destined to support B-47E forces for another ten months and further changes took place during the latter half of 1964, the 40th SAW at Brize Norton giving way to the 310th SAW in late June whilst at Upper Heyford the 380th SAW (redesignated from 380th BW on 15 September) surrendered its responsibility to the 310th SAW on 30 September. Thus, just before the end of 1964, the two remaining bases furnished support to three units, these being the 310th SAW which had aircraft at both, the 380th SAW at Brize Norton only and the 509th BW at Upper Heyford only. Subsequently, on 31 December 1964, the 310th SAW ceased its Reflex Action commitment, its B-47Es returning to Schilling AFB, Kansas, where the Wing wasted little time in disposing of its aircraft.

Thereafter, the 380th SAW and the 509th BW continued to perform nuclear alert duty until 31 March 1965 when they finally stood down. Within the next week, the 30 or so B-47Es which had been present at Brize Norton and Upper Heyford when the alert commitment was terminated, redeployed to the USA, bringing down the final curtain on Reflex Action in the United Kingdom just over seven years after this method of operation had begun.

Reflex Action was, of course, by no means confined to the United Kingdom, several other overseas bases being involved at various times. As noted earlier, this method of operation actually began at Sidi Slimane in Morocco on a trial basis in July 1957 and was soon extended to encompass the airfields at Ben Guerir

RIGHT
The last Stratojets to see regular operational use with the USAF were the WB-47Es of the Air Weather Service, represented here by 0-17063 at Elmendorf AFB, Alaska in October 1967. Surviving examples were retired to Davis-Monthan at the end of the decade
(Norman Taylor via Robert F Dorr)

BELOW
Trailing its deceleration and braking parachutes and minus the cockpit canopy, B-47E 20160 of the 509th Bomb Wing executes a perfect belly landing on a foam-covered runway at Pease AFB, New Hampshire in July 1965. An HH-43 Huskie rescue helicopter hovers nearby with fire-suppression equipment. This was not needed, and all crew members survived the incident without injury
(via Michael O'Leary)

and Nouasseur, B-47s from the 2nd, 19th, 305th, 306th, 308th, 321st and 379th Bomb Wings being amongst those which furnished aircraft to these bases between 1957 and July 1963 when Reflex Action simultaneously ceased at all three.

The same units plus the 384th BW and probably others almost certainly reflexed through the three Spanish bases at Moron, Torrejon, and Zaragoza, the latter airfield being the first to host B-47s when, in July 1957, 15 aircraft of the 40th BW were temporarily relocated from Greenham Common in order to participate in a brief exercise. As far as is known, none of these bases supported the 90-day rotational training programme but they were certainly heavily committed to 'Reflex Action', operations of this nature lasting for several years. Indeed, Moron and Torrejon did not bid farewell to the B-47 until the end of March 1965, operations from Zaragoza having been concluded just under one year earlier, in April 1964.

One other base known to have been intimately associated with Reflex Action was Elmendorf AFB, Alaska and this too remained active until the early part of 1965, units known to have deployed here including the 303rd BW from Davis-Monthan.

Andersen AFB, Guam also acted as a centre for continuously-rotating B-47s for a number of years

although, in this instance, the operation was code named 'Air Mail' and it was mainly supported by Bomb Wings situated at installations in the Western portion of the USA, these almost certainly including the 22nd and 320th BWs at March, the 9th BW/SAW at Mountain Home and the 43rd and 303rd BWs at Davis-Monthan. Aircraft engaged in Air Mail also performed ground alert in much the same way as Reflex Action, but the B-47's involvement in this activity eventually ceased in April 1964 when the B-52 assumed responsibility for this mission.

Changes in operating methods were by no means confined to overseas bases as earlier remarks about the introduction of the one-third alert programme will confirm although it is probably fair to say that, to a large extent, adoption of the revised alert concept and Reflex Action were synergistic in that the one could not have been easily accomplished without the other. That is not to say that the obstacles in maintaining the desired one-third alert level would have been insuperable had the 90-day rotational training programme continued but, certainly, the periodic upheaval that such deployments entailed would have unnecessarily complicated matters and it is generally acknowledged that logistical considerations played no small part in bringing about the revised methods of overseas operation.

Of greater significance, though, is the fact that the periodic change-over would inevitably have greatly impaired operational readiness and, in turn, seriously compromised the deterrent capability. By essentially eliminating this factor, Reflex Action permitted SAC to maintain a far higher percentage of its force in readiness than would otherwise have been the case and it was undoubtedly instrumental in enabling the Command to reach even higher levels of alert manning in later years.

Naturally, the increased alert posture dictated the need for additional combat-ready crews, SAC addressing this requirement in typical aggressive fashion by reassigning a couple of Strategic Reconnaissance Wings—the 70th and 90th SRWs—to the task of crew training during the spring and summer of 1958. In addition, reorganization of combat crew training procedures led to SAC gaining the McConnell-based 3520th Combat Crew Training Wing from Air Training Command on 1 July 1958 and it wasted little time in redesignating this as the 4347th CCTW. Even then, it took until May 1960 for SAC to achieve the desired level of one-third of all bomber and tanker assets on alert and this level had barely been achieved when the Command introduced yet another method of ensuring that sufficient bombers would survive in the event of a pre-emptive nuclear strike being mounted by the Soviet Union.

Dispersal of the B-52 fleet had, of course, been an active programme for some considerable time but little had been done as far as the still-large B-47 force

was concerned. Now, however, SAC turned its attentions to this matter, implementing a scheme whereby small numbers of Stratojets would be relocated to non-SAC bases and civilian airfields in times of crisis. Almost inevitably, this procedure was subjected to preliminary testing before being adopted on a widespread basis, perhaps the most notable occasion in which it was implemented in earnest being the Cuban Missile Crisis of October and November 1962 when fully-armed B-47s were despatched to numerous locations within the USA.

Dispersal in this manner offered a number of what might best be called 'benefits' although it is doubtful if those who resided close to the designated dispersal centres viewed the arrival of the B-47s with much relish. Nevertheless, it instantly compounded Soviet targeting problems whilst, with a great many extra runways available, it would also have enabled SAC to get a far larger proportion of the fleet airborne in a shorter interval, thus permitting the bomber force to remain an effective element of the deterrent. When one recalls that, for a time during the mid to late fifties, some SAC bases were home to two fully-fledged B-47 Bomb Wings (90 aircraft plus about 40 KC-97 tankers), it is perhaps surprising that it took such a long time to address the question of redistributing the Stratojet fleet. Reflex Action and the one-third alert obviously eased matters somewhat but these bases still represented attractive targets and in the event of a surprise attack, it is doubtful if more than a modest proportion could have got airborne

When the Stratojet finally reached the end of the line, the process of disposition was not simply a case of just cutting the aircraft up, these redundant airframes being a valuable source of useful spare parts. Some idea of the extent of reclamation undertaken on each B-47 can be gained from study of this photograph which shows just some of the items stripped from a surplus Stratojet at Davis-Monthan
(Col Albert Shower via Philip Chinnery)

Pictured soon after arrival at the Arizona storage facility, WB-E 0-15257 has still to be treated with preservative although the 'RECLM' inscription on the forward undercarriage door would seem to indicate that this aircraft was destined for early scrapping
(Lindsay Peacock)

before the bombs started falling.

Having only recently come fully 'up-to-speed' to achieve the one-third alert level, SAC was faced with a new challenge at the end of March 1961 when President Kennedy upped the ante by requesting that no less than 50 per cent of all bombers and tankers be held at 15-minutes readiness, a figure which was achieved in remarkably short order by July of the same year. However, this was something of a 'Catch-22' situation, for this demand was accompanied by the decision to accelerate the phase-out of the Stratojet to provide sufficient trained crews to meet increased alert commitments, no less than five Bomb Wings disposing of the B-47 in 1961. As it turned out, some units received a reprieve in late July when heightening tension over the Berlin situation prompted the President to revise his earlier decree, six B-47 Wings being granted an extended lease of life as a result of an understandable desire to enhance deterrent capability, at least until additional ICBMs attained operational status.

In point of fact, withdrawal of the B-47 had begun some considerable time before, when, in January 1959, the Biggs-based 97th BW disposed of its aircraft in anticipation of receiving the B-52 Stratofortress whilst, in the summer of that same year, the 308th BW was reduced to a manning level of just one officer and one airman in order to provide

additional B-47Es so as to bring the two so-called 'super-strength' Wings at Hunter, Georgia (2nd BW) and Plattsburgh, New York (380th BW) up to a level of 70 aircraft each.

Further force reductions followed in 1960 when the 43rd, 44th and 320th BWs all ceased operations although the former unit was perhaps luckier than most in that it re-equipped with Convair's remarkable B-58A Hustler, in the process becoming the first of only two units destined to employ this machine operationally. Further substantial cuts in the size of the B-47 fleet occurred during 1961 when both of the Homestead-based Wings (19th and 379th) ceased operations pending re-equipment with the B-52 whilst the 305th BW followed in the footsteps of the 43rd BW and converted to the B-58A. Two more Wings—the 321st and 341st—were less fortunate in that they were both inactivated.

Thereafter, the Berlin crisis of 1961 and the Cuban missile crisis of 1962 were major contributory factors in delaying the phase-out and, indeed, only one Wing—the 70th BW—fell by the wayside in 1962, this being untypical in that it had only recently been redesignated following reassignment from crew training to bomber tasks and had not attained combat ready status at the time of inactivation in June 1962.

In fact, the crises of 1961–62 represented only a temporary stay of execution for the units concerned, and, once the dust had settled, the phase-out process was resumed with renewed vigour in 1963. Six Wings—the 2nd, 22nd, 68th, 306th and 340th BWs plus the 96th SAW—all disappeared from the scene during that year whilst 1964 witnessed the demise of four more, these comprising the 40th SAW and the 301st, 303rd and 384th BWs.

Thus, at the start of the last full calendar year of B-47 operations, only eight Wings remained active and some of those had begun to wind-down as the retirement process moved into its final phase. In the event, the 307th BW, the 310th SAW and the 376th BW had disposed of their B-47s by the summer of 1965 but the final nail in the coffin came in early October when Project Fast Fly was implemented. This had as its primary objective the accelerated disposition of the five remaining Wings and essentially brought forward the targetted deadline of June 1966 for the eventual phase-out by some six months.

Boeing's Stratojet clearly dominated this parking area at Davis-Monthan, many of the 1,000 aircraft that were committed for storage being visible. The long shed-like structure which can be clearly seen in the middle distance is the main reclamation facility while other types in evidence include Douglas Invaders, Douglas Skyraiders, Lockheed T-33s, Boeing B-50s, Boeing C-97s, Fairchild C-119s and Douglas C-47s
(USAF via Lindsay Peacock)

Accordingly, the 98th SAW, the 380th SAW and the 509th BW began to dispose of their aircraft more or less immediately, a task which was completed before the end of 1965 while the last day of that year marked the end of an era when the 9th SAW and the 100th BW relinquished their ground alert obligations. All that now remained was for these two Wings to consign their Stratojets to storage at Davis-Monthan, a task which was eventually completed on 11 February 1966 when SAC's last two B-47Es— 36235 of the 9th SAW at Mountain Home AFB, Idaho and 32286 of the 100th BW at Pease AFB, New Hampshire—flew into retirement. 'Fast Fly' was complete but the Stratojet lingered on. . .

B-47s and B-52s are visible in this view of part of the storage area at Davis-Monthan. Unlike the B-52—some examples of which were held in storage for more than 15 years—the B-47 was disposed of quite quickly, almost all of the 1,000 or so Stratojets which found their way here being scrapped in the late 1960s
(USAF via Philip Chinnery)

Chapter 9
The Intelligence Game

In addition to the standard bomber variants of the Stratojet, SAC also acquired a substantial number of reconnaissance-dedicated machines. Three models were new-build aircraft, these being the RB-47E, the RB-47H and the RB-47K. Of these three sub-types, the RB-47E theoretically had a secondary bomber role although this appears to have been viewed by most as being basically a latent capability. In addition to the purpose-built versions mentioned above, SAC also acquired a fairly substantial number of YRB-47Bs, this being a variant which might best be described as a stop-gap conversion and one which appears to have also been known as the RB-47B.

As far as the YRB-47B conversions were concerned, these came about primarily as a result of slippage with the specialist RB-47E model, it being apparent by March 1952 that the definitive photographic-reconnaissance version would be unlikely to attain operational capability until some time in 1954. Rather than delay the transition programme, it was decided to fit camera pods to approximately 90 B-47Bs (aircraft numbers 90 to 180) so as to permit a couple of Strategic Reconnaissance Wings to achieve an initial operating capacity rather earlier than would otherwise have been possible. These aircraft would utilize the temporary designation YRB-47B until such time as they reverted to pure bomber configuration and it is understood that they incorporated a special bomb bay package consisting of eight cameras.

The first two units to acquire the YRB-47B were both stationed at Lockbourne AFB, Ohio, deliveries of the interim aircraft getting under way in May 1953 when the 91st SRW received its first example. Subsequently, in September of the same year, the co-located 26th SRW also acquired some examples of the YRB-47B and both units continued to operate this type until 1954 when sufficient RB-47Es were available to permit re-equipment.

This, however, did not mark the end of the YRB-47B in SAC service for two Bomb Wings are also known to have operated this type. At March AFB, California, the 320th Bomb Wing had some of these machines during the course of 1953–54, this unit being tasked in the dual bomber and reconnaissance roles for a short time whilst others are known to have been active with the 340th Bomb Wing at Sedalia AFB, Missouri in 1954–55, these probably being assigned to facilitate the process of working up to fully operational status with the B-47.

With some 240 examples being completed by Boeing-Wichita between March 1953 and August 1955, the RB-47E was easily the most numerous reconnaissance derivative and it eventually saw operational service with five Strategic Reconnaissance Wings between 1953 and 1961. As already noted, both the 26th and 91st SRWs were initially equipped with the interim YRB-47B but both progressed to the definitive RB-47E during the course of 1954.

Two more units—both resident at Forbes—also acquired the RB-47E during 1954, these being the 55th SRW (ex RB-50) and the 90th SRW (ex RB-29) while the final Wing was the 70th SRW at Little Rock, this being a 'new' unit which was organised during the course of 1955. In the event, the RB-47E does not appear to have been quite so successful as the B-47 and it subsequently became the first example of the breed to begin to disappear from the inventory, the process of withdrawal getting under way as early as October 1957. At its peak in 1956, however, SAC had an RB-47 fleet which slightly exceeded the 250 mark, which, while pretty small beer when compared with the number of straight B-47s, was by no means insignificant.

As far as reconnaissance-dedicated variants of the Stratojet were concerned, the RB-47H appears to have been the most successful and it was certainly the

By far the most numerous reconnaissance version of the
Stratojet was the RB-47E, some 240 aircraft being
completed for service with five Strategic Reconnaissance
Wings. Assigned primarily to photographic tasks, they soon
began to disappear from the inventory and the first
examples were dispatched for storage in 1957. Here, late
production RB-47E 34262 takes fuel from a KC-97F and
it should be noted that this Stratojet lacks the integral
RATO installation
(Boeing via Michael O'Leary)

most durable, remaining in service long after the RB-47E and RB-47K were withdrawn. Basically concerned with electronic surveillance—a potentially hazardous task which included the so-called 'ferret' mission—it was built in only modest quantities, a total of 35 being completed for service with two squadrons of the 55th SRW, some of which may actually have been produced to ERB-47H configuration. In its original guise, deliveries began in the latter half of 1955 and continued into 1956, this model eventually gaining the distinction of being the last variant of the Stratojet to see active service with SAC and it was not until December 1967 that the last example was finally retired from service by the 55th SRW which had, in the interval, moved from Forbes to Offutt where it eventually re-equipped with the RC-135C.

The remaining variant assigned to tasks of a reconnaissance nature was the RB-47K, 15 examples being delivered in 1955–56 to equip a single squadron of the 55th SRW at Forbes. These were primarily concerned with the weather reconnaissance mission and some remained active until the summer of 1963 when the 338th SRS was inactivated, the RB-47Ks previously assigned being placed in storage and eventually sold for scrap.

Aircraft dedicated to strategic reconnaissance—seemingly a catch-all terminology encompassing a variety of missions and a multitude of sins—also undertook rotational training duty along similar lines to those employed by SAC's Bomb Wings, especially

during the 1955–56 period. Instances of Wing-sized deployments made by SRWs include a 45-day TDY to Upper Heyford by the 26th SRW in September and October 1954 whilst the 55th SRW is known to have spent three months at Ben Guerir, Morocco, in the summer of 1955 and the 90th SRW completed an even longer tour of duty at Eielson AFB, Alaska, also in summer 1955.

In addition, extensive use was made of detachments, small numbers of aircraft appearing from time to time at some of the British bases for periods of temporary residence which varied in duration from a matter of a few days to months. These usually dropped in more or less unheralded and invariably went about their business quietly—or, at least, as quietly as was possible with something as visible as the RB-47—and with a minimum of fuss before departing almost as mysteriously as they had arrived and it seems reasonable to assume that similar detachments were to be seen at other overseas SAC bases. Ultimately, the 55th SRW became the acknowledged masters of this method of operation, maintaining detachments—some of which were virtually permanent—at numerous locations around the world.

Changing requirements with regard to SAC war plans and a diminishing need for manned photographic reconnaissance capability conspired to ren-

LEFT
Aircraft of the 55th SRW pursued a particularly nomadic existence as they went about their primary mission of acquiring electronic intelligence. This task was not without hazard as the crew of an RB-47H operating from Brize Norton learned in 1960 when they were shot down by Soviet fighters. Here, ERB-47H 0-36249 departs from Brize Norton accompanied by tell-tale black smoke (Aviation Photo News)

BELOW
Unlike their pure bomber counterparts, the RB-47Hs of the 55th Strategic Reconnaissance Wing seemed to conform to no precise pattern of deployment, coming and going at frequent but always unpredictable intervals as they went about their work of gathering electronic intelligence on a global basis. One base which did support a 55th SRW detachment for a number of years was Brize Norton, where RB-47H 0-34298 was photographed in the early 1960s while on temporary duty (TDY) from Forbes AFB, Kansas (Aviation Photo News)

der the RB-47E more or less obsolescent in a very short space of time with the inevitable result that the process of retirement got under way as early as 14 October 1957, less than two years after the last example had been delivered to the Command. On that date, the 91st SRW at Lockbourne began to despatch its RB-47Es to the storage facility at Davis-Monthan AFB, Arizona, the first machine to be retired being 15272. A little over three weeks later, on 8 November, the 91st SRW was inactivated and it was soon followed into limbo by the 26th SRW which completed transfer of its RB-47Es in mid-April 1958 although it was not deactivated until 1 July of that year. Subsequently, the two surviving RB-47E Wings were reassigned to crew training tasks as part of the measures taken to ensure that SAC had sufficient combat-ready crews to support the revised alert procedures that were adopted during 1958. In the case of the Little Rock-based 70th SRW, this switched from reconnaissance to crew training in mid-June 1958, having been preceded just a month earlier by the 90th SRW at Forbes.

Thus, by the summer of 1958, SAC retained just one fully operational medium SRW, this being the 55th at Forbes but even here the situation had changed dramatically, in that the delivery of 35 examples of the RB-47H in 1955–56 had enabled this Wing to resume its earlier task of electronic reconnaissance. In addition to the RB-47H, the 55th SRW also acquired 15 examples of the RB-47K at about the same time, employing these for weather reconnaissance, a task that was performed by the 338th SRS whilst the 38th and 343rd SRSs utilised the RB-47Hs.

Despite only being equipped with the RB-47E for little more than a year, the 55th had nevertheless managed to secure top honours in the fourth navigation and reconnaissance competition which was held at Lockbourne AFB, Ohio, in September 1955, barely a month after the Wing returned from overseas duty at Ben Guerir. Pitted against four other RB-47E Wings, the 55th turned in the best overall performance to earn the coveted P T Cullen award. Thereafter, the 55th turned its attentions to preparing to move back into the electronic intelligence business in a big way and it had received the first RB-47Hs by the end of 1955, the process of transition extending until well into 1956.

The very nature of the mission performed by 55th SRW aircraft and the fact that it was one of only a handful of units so engaged almost inevitably dictated that operations were conducted on a truly global scale with a considerable amount of Wing resources being deployed overseas at any given time. Indeed, in many respects, the 55th's existence was highly nomadic for, in addition to the headquarters elements at Forbes, it maintained near-permanent detachments or operating locations at several overseas bases.

Not surprisingly, since it was viewed as being the most likely aggressor, the Soviet Union featured prominently in the intelligence-gathering effort but there can be little doubt that such activities were by no means confined to that country and, indeed, unofficial historical studies do confirm that the 55th SRW also directed its attentions to such countries as North Korea, North Vietnam and the People's Republic of China.

Further oblique confirmation of the 55th's global intelligence-gathering activity is provided by a number of well-publicised incidents involving aircraft known to have been assigned to this Wing, RB-47Hs being subjected to vigorous and determined opposition which occasionally had tragic results. In such instances, SAC headquarters generally maintained a fairly dignified posture, choosing to shelter behind tight-lipped silence and neither giving credence to nor denying the often speculative and frequently wildly inaccurate press reports. In reality, however, such incidents probably represented only the tip of the iceberg, the strict security blanket which cloaked 55th SRW operations being permitted to slip only rarely.

Since much of the 55th's energies were directed at detecting, monitoring, classifying and recording Soviet radar and electronic emissions, it is hardly surprising that most of the permanent overseas detachments were located reasonably close to the various areas which merited particularly close and near-continuous surveillance.

For much of the Stratojet era, the 55th SRW maintained a permanent presence in Alaska, Eng-

TOP RIGHT

RB-47Hs and ERB-47Hs of the 55th SRW never adopted white anti-flash undersides, this presumably being partly a weight-saving measure and partly in recognition of the fact that they were not configured to deliver nuclear weapons. The aircraft depicted here at Brize Norton, ERB-47H 0-36249, is historically significant by virtue of being the very last Stratojet to be produced by the parent company at Wichita. It was delivered to SAC in early 1957 (Aviation Photo News)

RIGHT

Streaming its deceleration chute, RB-47H 0-34286 of the 55th SRW returns to Brize Norton at the end of an intelligence-gathering mission in 1964. Numerous antenna fairings can be seen in the area of the aft fuselage and this aircraft also carries the ALD-4 pod. As far as unit markings were concerned, 55th SRW aircraft are not known to have displayed the wing badge, although some RB-47s were noted with SAC's badge on the nose section (John Hughes)

land, Greenland, Japan and Turkey whilst operations were also conducted from numerous other facilities at various times, these encompassing such bases as Clark in the Philippines; Bien Hoa and Da Nang in South Vietnam; Osan, Korea; Bodo, Norway; Athens, Greece; Torrejon, Spain and Shemya in the Aleutian Islands. As far as the permanent detachments were concerned, with the exception of Turkey, they were always modestly sized, generally consisting of just one or two aircraft and crews, with periodic changeovers taking place although there appears to have been no set rotational pattern.

In England, Detachment One operated for many years, primarily from Brize Norton although other bases—most notably Upper Heyford—also supported RB-47H and ERB-47H activities and, indeed, the latter facility served as home to Det 1 during the last few years of the Stratojet era.

As is the case with all overseas operations, details relating to the primary area of interest are sketchy to say the least although some clues were furnished by the much-publicised shooting down of RB-47H 34281 by a Soviet MiG interceptor on 1 July 1960. Operating from Brize Norton, four members of the six-man crew lost their lives in this incident which apparently took place over the Barents Sea in the vicinity of the Kola Peninsula.

As had been the case just two months earlier when a U-2 flown by Francis 'Gary' Powers was brought down, the Soviet authorities waited a while before revealing on 11 July that they had been responsible for the destruction of the RB-47H which they insisted had penetrated Russian airspace and that they had taken the two surviving crewmen prisoner. As far as the USA was concerned, this episode could hardly have come at a more highly charged moment and, as usual, Soviet Premier Nikita Kruschev was not slow to denounce the Americans. Subsequently, on 25 January 1961, the two survivors—Captains Freeman Olmstead and John McKone—were released after spending several months incarcerated in Moscow's infamous Lubyanka prison.

On the other side of the world, Yokota AB in Japan hosted the 55th SRW's Detachment Two, prime areas of responsibility almost certainly including the Kamchatka Peninsula, the Sea of Okhotsk and, now probably most infamous of all following the recent shooting down of a Korean Air Lines Boeing 747, Sakhalin Island. However, in view of its close proximity, it seems highly unlikely that the People's Republic of China would have escaped surveillance whilst North Korea also came in for some attention, this being confirmed in dramatic fashion in late April 1965 when an RB-47H came under fire from a pair of North Korean MiG-17s.

On this occasion, however, the Stratojet was able to fend off its attackers and return to Yokota, the twin 20-mm tail cannon carried by the RB-47H playing no small part in ensuring its survival. Nevertheless, the aircraft concerned was badly damaged during the course of what was described as a 'furious engagement', two engines being put out of action whilst a third was only able to operate at reduced power. In addition, hydraulic and other key systems suffered extensive damage and the ensuing flapless landing at Yokota was only accomplished with difficulty. Happily, none of the six crew members sustained injury in this engagement but the degree of damage inflicted on the RB-47H ultimately resulted in it being stricken from the inventory and scrapped.

Detachment Three was located at Eielson AFB, Alaska, approximately 30 miles (48 km) from Fairbanks and a pretty unpleasant place to be in winter when temperatures regularly fell to 60 below. Again, the principal area of interest remains shrouded in secrecy but it seems reasonable to assume that the Bering Strait was regularly overflown, RB-47Hs possibly covering the North-Eastern portion of the USSR from the relative security of the Chukchi and East Siberian Seas.

However, missions from Eielson almost certainly covered a far greater area than just this small portion of the Soviet Union, an inference which tends to be supported by the fact that crews were on occasion

tasked to overfly the North Pole and it was during one such sortie that a particularly amusing incident occurred.

Having left the 'target' area for their return to Eielson via the North Pole, the RB-47H crew involved reached the conclusion that performing a tight 360 degree turn above the Polar region would qualify for consideration as a new record for a round-the-world flight in the shortest possible time. This they duly did but about half-way through the turn, the copilot reported seeing a light on the ground.

Further circuits followed, the landing lights being used to signal whatever or whoever it was that lay below, each signal eliciting a response but it was to be another 24 hours or so before the 55th crew learned that, quite by chance, they had been flying overhead when the nuclear-powered submarine USS Sargo had surfaced at the Pole after spending six hazardous weeks beneath the ice cap. Naturally, the RB-47H crew reported this odd incident and this was subsequently forwarded to SAC headquarters with the remainder of the post-mission report, enabling SAC to score a few points by despatching a message which read 'position of Sargo confirmed . . . SAC' to the Chief of Naval Operations shortly after the

official announcement was made.

In distinct contrast to the chill of Alaska, Detachment Four enjoyed a rather more pleasant climate, being located at Incirlik in Turkey, this base being home to a fairly substantial portion of 55th SRW assets for several years in the late fifties and early sixties. In addition to the 'standard' RB-47Hs, Incirlik also supported a little-known aspect of 55th SRW activities, three specially configured examples of the Stratojet known as EB-47E(TT)s being employed to monitor the Soviet space and missile centre at Tyuratam and, almost certainly, the Intermediate Range Ballistic Missile (IRBM) test facility at Kapustin Yar, an operation which required the presence of four crews so that one might be held on alert at all times.

Some of the long-haul missions staged by RB-47Hs operating with Detachment Five from Thule, Greenland, required inflight refuelling support from as many as nine examples of the Boeing KC-97G Stratofreighter if the objective was to be achieved. Later, the availability of the jet-powered KC-135A Stratotanker made life slightly easier
(Aviation Photo News)

LEFT
Following the closure of Brize Norton as a SAC base, Detachment One transferred its activities to nearby Upper Heyford. RB-47Hs and ERB-47Hs continued to operate from here until the summer of 1967, the subject of this picture—RB-47H 0-34280—being the last of the 'ferrets' to be seen in England. The ALD-4 pod is clearly visible at the side of the centre fuselage section
(Paul Bennett)

BELOW
Almost certainly taken soon after arrival at Davis-Montham, RB-47H 0-34296 was of particular historical significance in that it was SAC's very last Stratojet, being retired by the 55th SRW on 29 December 1967. Showing little sign of the physical deterioration which generally accompanied prolonged periods of storage, '296 spent only a relatively brief period with the Military Aircraft Storage and Disposition center, being restored to flying status fairly soon afterwards and assigned to the testing of F-111 avionics equipment. One of the last Stratojets to remain in airworthy condition, it spent several years at Los Angeles Air Force Station adjacent to the international airport before ultimately finding its way to Eglin AFB, Florida, where it apparently still resides as a museum exhibit
(via Robert F Dorr)

Allocated the code-name 'Iron Work', this operation seems to have begun in earnest during the course of 1958, the 'Tell-Two' Stratojets assigned to this task all being modified bombers. At least two different 'Tell-Two' configurations have been identified, with both featuring a bomb bay capsule to accommodate the two 'Ravens' (Electronic Warfare Officers) carried by this variant. As far as the electronics package is concerned, little hard information has come to light but, like the RB-47Hs, this almost certainly changed during the period of 'Iron Work' operations as more sophisticated equipment became available.

At least one of the EB-47E(TT)s (32316) carried a form of 'towel-rail' antenna on either side of the nose section forward of the cockpit, whilst 32320 featured prominent SLAR (side-looking airborne radar) pods on both sides of the fore and aft fuselage. Details of the configuration and identity of the third aircraft are not readily available but it is known that one of the trio (32320) was destroyed when it crashed and burned with two fatalities while attempting to land at Incirlik in the autumn of 1962.

Anyone who is familiar with the 55th SRW will probably be aware of the fact that this unit has on several occasions in the past indulged in 're-numbering' its aircraft, presumably in an attempt to mislead onlookers. However, from time to time, they get it badly wrong, a classic instance occurring a few years back when an RC-135 turned up at Mildenhall with a 'serial number' which lay outside the correct serial block. Naturally, local enthusiasts were hugely amused by this effort to deceive but there were probably red faces elsewhere when it became apparent that this simple attempt at subterfuge had succeeded only in drawing attention to the RC-135.

A similar sort of game was played with the 'Tell-Two' Stratojets when the 55th SRW first received these aircraft, although this time serial numbers were not applied at all. Not surprisingly, this caused a certain amount of confusion which probably reached a peak when two of the EB-47Es were sharing hangar space. One of the pair was slated to undergo an engine change and, needless to say, it was not until after this task had been completed that study of the relevant paperwork revealed that the engine change had in fact been carried out on the wrong aircraft.

In addition to the 'Tell-Two' aircraft, Incirlik also served as a centre for the more usual 55th SRW mission of acquiring electronic intelligence, examples of the RB-47H and the much rarer ERB-47H being stationed here to cover the southern border of the USSR.

The other long-lived permanent overseas operating location was Thule, Greenland, which was home to Detachment Five, this inhospitable outpost being—if such a thing were possible—even less attractive than Eielson. Certainly, missions from Thule were far more demanding in that each featured a long trans-polar flight before the area of interest was even reached and once the necessary task was performed the crew then faced an equally long transit back to base. In-flight refuelling support was essential to the success of the missions staged from Thule, the pair of temporarily resident RB-47Hs normally sharing the flight line with no fewer than ten examples of the KC-97.

Planning was meticulous for, with many missions requiring the support of no less than nine KC-97s, timing was of paramount importance. In practice, it was usual for tankers to depart in cells well in advance of the RB-47 which had to rendezvous successfully with eight KC-97s in order to receive enough fuel to accomplish the task, whilst it was by no means unknown for further fuel transfers to take place on the return journey. The availability of sufficient KC-135 Stratotankers to permit assignment of this type to the Thule-based Tanker Task Force made life slightly easier in that fewer support aircraft were required but operational missions from here—and, for the matter, anywhere else—were always demanding by virtue of the fact that they were invariably undertaken in conditions of strict radio silence. Since it was not uncommon to be intercepted by fighter aircraft flown by a potential adversary and since it was not always easy to gauge their intentions, it follows automatically that such encounters must have heightened the feeling of isolation. Nevertheless, it was policy only to abort missions when hostile intent was apparent, a somewhat vague ruling which gave the aircraft commander a fair amount of latitude when it came to determining what could be construed as 'hostile intent'.

Indeed, it was this very question which gave rise to one amusing tale when the Defense Intelligence Agency (DIA) received a package of mission material containing a still picture showing a MiG-19 flying in formation just a few feet from the port wing-tip of an RB-47H. Their immediate reaction on seeing this picture was to query SAC headquarters as to why the mission wasn't aborted. SAC duly replied with the comment that aborts only occurred when 'hostile intent' was apparent, to which the DIA countered with something along the lines of 'how do you determine a pilot's intentions when you let him get so close?' As usual, SAC seem to have had the last word, responding with the simple message 'by the expression on the pilot's face'.

In 1965, however, the extent of RB-47H operations began to wind down, one of the two squadrons which utilized this mark—the 38th SRS—departing to Offutt AFB, Nebraska, where it acquired responsibility for SAC's 'Looking Glass' airborne command post EC-135Cs. Subsequently, the 343rd SRS was reunited with the 38th in the summer of 1966 when the 55th SRW was officially relocated to Offutt, this squadron continuing to use the RB-47H until 25 March 1967, when, following the delivery of the first RC-135Cs, it turned over the remaining Stratojets to the newly-reactivated 338th SRS.

During the early to mid 1960s, variants of the C-135 initially supplanted and eventually replaced the RB-47H as the prime intelligence-gathering tool. These are represented by RC-135D 00357 at RAF Mildenhall in the late 1960s
(via Lindsay Peacock)

By then, of course, the extent of RB-47H activity had diminished greatly, especially with regard to overseas bases. For instance, Det 2 at Yokota ceased to employ the type in early January 1967, the last major operation accomplished from here being 'Box Top', this code name almost certainly referring to the acquisition of electronic intelligence pertaining to North Vietnam.

Elsewhere, Det 1—by now at Upper Heyford—continued to host the Stratojet for a few months longer, the last confirmed sighting here occurring in June 1967 when RB-47H 34280 was noted. Thereafter, the task of gathering electronic intelligence was entrusted to various marks of the RC-135.

With the type having been more or less completely withdrawn from overseas service by the summer of 1967, the end was clearly in sight. Nevertheless, it was not until 29 December 1967 that the very last SAC Stratojet was formally retired from service, an event which was predated by the inactivation of the 338th SRS on Christmas Day. The aircraft concerned—RB-47H 34296—duly took its place alongside approximately 1,000 other Stratojets in the huge storage facility at Davis-Monthan AFB, Arizona but, unlike most, '296 was not destined to remain there for long, being rescued from the 'bone-yard' and given a new lease of life testing F-111 avionics equipment fairly soon afterwards.

Chapter 10
The End of the Line

Following the retirement of SAC's last Stratojet at the end of 1967, it was all pretty much a downhill story for the number of aircraft which remained active steadily diminished as the decade progressed.

By far the greater majority of flyable aircraft were the WB-47E 'weather birds' which served with MAC (Military Airlift Command), an organization which had come into being on 1 January 1966 when it inherited those assets previously assigned to MATS. Operated by that command's Air Weather Service, the WB-47E was still employed in an operational capacity as the seventies dawned but the process of retirement had already begun, the first examples of this sub-type having been consigned to the 'bone-yard' at Davis-Monthan during the closing stages of 1969.

Once the phase-out process got under way in earnest, it did not take long to be completed, the last WB-47Es disappearing from the inventory during the course of 1970. As usual most found their way to MASDC where they were to spend the next few years in virtual splendid isolation before eventually being sold for scrap. Sadly, of the 1,000-plus B-47s and RB-47s which had preceded them into storage, by the end of 1969 little remained, these having fallen victim to what can only be described as an orgy of destruction. Most were cut-up during 1968, the task of scrapping being accomplished on base by outside contractors.

Other Stratojets which continued to perform useful, if largely unnoticed, tasks during the late sixties included a pair of vividly-marked QB-47E drones (34256 and 34263) with the 3214th OMS at Eglin but these too headed west for storage during the course of 1968, a year which also marked the final flights of a couple of other long-serving machines. At Kirtland AFB in New Mexico, B-47E 32276 undertook a variety of test duties with the Air Force Special Weapons Center until 19 February 1968 when it too was retired, having been replaced by an

early production example of the B-52 Stratofortress, whilst, some way to the North, JB-47E 32280 of the Air Force Systems Command's Aeronautical Systems Division at Wright-Patterson AFB, Ohio also came to the end of its flying career at about this time, this having formed part of the 4950th Test Wing's diverse fleet of aircraft.

By the beginning of 1971, literally only a handful of the 2,042 Stratojets built were still actively flying and three of those were actually operated by the US Navy, one (32104) being the well-known 'seven-engined' NB-47E which was employed to test the General Electric TF34-GE-2 turbofan engine selected to power the Lockheed S-3A Viking. Operating from Edwards AFB, California for much of 1971, this carried the test engine on a pylon beneath the port wing roughly mid-way between the existing J47 pods but once the prototype S-3A itself took to the air in January 1972 this aircraft's useful life more or less came to an end and it soon found its way to storage at

Operated by the 301st and 376th BWs at various times, EB-47E 32135 is one of the few aircraft to have escaped the cutter's axe at Davis-Monthan. It now forms part of the impressively large Pima Air Museum collection (Lindsay Peacock)

TOP LEFT
*Positioned close to the golf course at Davis-Monthan,
former 9th Strategic Aerospace Wing B-47E 0-36196
certainly constituted a most unusual hazard when
photographed in November 1969. One of the few Stratojets
which survived the orgy of scrapping in the late 1960s,
'196 has, sadly, since been broken up*
(Lindsay Peacock)

ABOVE
*At the end of its Navy flying career, NB-47E 0-32104
also found its way to Davis-Monthan. Unlike many former
inmates, it managed to escape and now forms part of a
museum collection in Pueblo, Colorado*
(via Lindsay Peacock)

LEFT
*The MASDC park number '41B007' on the forward
undercarriage door helps to identify this Stratojet as the
former NB-47E 32104. Carrying the civil registration
N1045X on the aft fuselage and with all other markings
erased, it was almost certainly photographed in the summer
of 1979 while in process of being transferred to Pueblo.
Rather interestingly, it appears to have gained SAC's star-
spangled sash whilst in store*
(Brian Rogers)

*End of the line! Taken on an
uncharacteristically gloomy day, this view
of the desert storage facility at Davis-
Monthan shows some of the 1,000-plus
Stratojets which were consigned here for
storage and ultimate destruction. Exactly
350 aircraft are visible in the foreground,
further concentrations of B-47s being
discernible in the distance*
(via Philip Chinnery)

TOP LEFT
Journey's end. NB-47E 32104 at its final resting-place in Colorado. Markings on the forward fuselage section are most definitely non-standard while the civil registration is still present behind the national insignia
(via Robert F Dorr)

ABOVE
The SAC Museum at Offutt AFB, Nebraska naturally features one example of the Stratojet in what is an impressive collection of artifacts. Built by Douglas, B-47E 21412 displays the badge of the 301st Bomb Wing on the nose section
(Lindsay Peacock)

LEFT
By November 1969 little evidence of SAC's once-proud fleet of Stratojets was to be seen at Davis-Monthan. Apart from a handful of B-47Es, two or three RB-47Hs were the only former SAC aircraft in store. Ex-55th SRW RB-47H 0-34302 was one of the latter and was liberally coated in 'spraylat' preservative. By the autumn of 1973 it had been scrapped
(Lindsay Peacock)

177

TOP LEFT
Displaying the badge of the 96th Bomb Wing on the nose section, B-47E 2412 'guards the gate' at Dyess AFB, Texas. One of the last Stratojets to fly regularly, it served with the Navy's Fleet Electronic Warfare Support Group as an EB-47E until about 1977. Whilst active with the Navy it carried the tail number 24120, a corruption of its official serial number
(Chris Ryan)

ABOVE
Part of the US Air Force Museum collection, B-47E-135-BW 36244 is historically significant by virtue of being the last pure bomber Stratojet to be produced by the parent company. After service with SAC's 307th Bomb Wing, it was retired to Wright-Patterson AFB, Ohio, where it still resides today
(via Lindsay Peacock)

LEFT
B-47E-25-DT 20166 looked decidedly the worse for wear when photographed in company with others of its kind at the Naval Weapons Center at China Lake, California in April 1974. Happily, this particular Stratojet still survives, having been transferred to join the rapidly expanding collection of historic aircraft at Castle AFB, California
(Peter R Foster)

Davis-Monthan. Several years later, in the summer of 1979, it was briefly restored to flying condition and given the temporary civil registration N1045X for a one-way flight to Pueblo, Colorado where it was to form part of a museum collection.

The other two Navy machines were the pair of EB-47Es which flew from Tulsa, Oklahoma on a variety of electronics-based duties under the auspices of the Fleet Electronic Warfare Support Group (FEWSG), Douglas being responsible for furnishing mainten-ance support and physically operating these aircraft under the terms of a US Navy contract. Much of the work undertaken was of an 'aggressor' nature, the EB-47Es being employed to evaluate the capability of Navy air and sea forces to conduct effective operations in an intense ECM environment but some test work was also undertaken and both Stratojets acquired a variety of external 'growths' whilst employed on FEWSG tasks. Eventually, their capacity to adapt to this quite demanding mission declined and after some ten years of service they were finally replaced by a pair of suitably modified NKC-

135A Stratotankers during the course of 1977.

The only other Stratojet which survived to the mid-seventies in a flyable condition was in fact the very last example to be retired by SAC, namely RB-47H 34296. Initially consigned to storage at MASDC, this was soon granted a reprieve and following refurbishment it returned to flying duties with the Space and Missile Systems Organization's 6592nd ABG at Los Angeles AFS, California. Operating from a small compound on the perimeter of Los Angeles International Airport, '296 was quite extensively modified, acquiring, for instance, a needle nose as part of a project concerned with testing F-111 avionics. Underwing pods were also installed for a while as part of this project whilst at a later date the undersurfaces were painted white, making it truly unique for no other RB-47H ever had white undersides. Eventually, though, time caught up with 34296 which ceased flying at about the same time as the FEWSG EB-47Es. When last heard of, this Stratojet was at Eglin in non-flyable condition, the needle nose having been replaced by one which

appeared to have been taken from a standard B-47E, giving it a most odd appearance.

Although by far the greater majority of Stratojets ended their days at Davis-Monthan, a modest number did escape the tender mercies of the scrap merchants and quite a few have earned honourable retirement either as gate guardians or as museum pieces. Of these, by far the most significant is the second XB-47 (46-66) which can still be seen today at Chanute AFB, Illinois although its colour scheme is far from authentic and its real identity is in fact not readily apparent, the serial number on the fin being given as '2278' which was, of course, a Lockheed-built B-47E.

Other historically less significant examples can be found in Arkansas, California, Kansas, Louisiana, Nebraska and Oklahoma whilst the USAF Museum collection at Wright-Patterson AFB, Ohio features the very last B-47E to be built (53-6244) as its sole representative of this type.

One of the few 'weather birds' to survive, WB-47E 0-17066 now resides not too far from the Stratojet's original birthplace in Seattle, Washington, being preserved at Boeing Field
(Douglas M Remington)

Acknowledgements

In preparing this volume, I am indebted to many people who have provided snippets of information over a considerable period of time but who will have to be content with going unrecognized since a full listing would probably cover several pages. However, the following do deserve acknowledgement by virtue of having made a significant contribution to the content. While being generous in acknowledging their assistance, I suppose I cannot really expect them to share the blame in the event of any errors or inaccuracies becoming apparent.

Leaving aside the matter of brickbats and bouquets, Graham Luxton's contribution was particularly valuable for it was he who took on the onerous task of reading the original manuscript, following up with many suggestions and much information which materially improved the finished article. Chris Pocock also perused parts of the manuscript and provided valuable insight into certain areas of the Stratojet saga.

Turning to illustrative material, individual photographers are naturally credited throughout but I am indebted to Paul Bennett, Philip Chinnery, Robert F Dorr, John Hughes, Michael O'Leary, and Barry Wheeler for assistance in this often troublesome area, for, despite the fact that over 2,000 examples of the B-47 and RB-47 were built, there seems to be a dearth of readily available material.

Finally, I'd like to thank all those who were generous enough to 'share a ride' back in the early sixties, when, in company with a number of 'fellow travellers', I took to making weekly hitch-hiking expeditions to the SAC bases—had it not been for them, I doubt if this book would ever have been written.

Glossary

AAF	Army Air Field
AB	Air Base
AD	Air Division
AFB	Air Force Base
AFS	Air Force Station
ARS	Air Refuelling Squadron
ARW	Air Refuelling Wing
AWS	Air Weather Service
BG	Bomb Group
BG(M)	Bomb Group (Medium)
BS	Bomb Squadron
BS(H)	Bomb Squadron (Heavy)
BS(L)	Bomb Squadron (Light)
BS(M)	Bomb Squadron (Medium)
BS(VH)	Bomb Squadron (Very Heavy)
BW	Bomb Wing
BW(H)	Bomb Wing (Heavy)
BW(M)	Bomb Wing (Medium)
CCTS	Combat Crew Training Squadron
CCTW	Combat Crew Training Wing
ConUS	Continental USA
ECM	Electronic Countermeasures
EWO	Electronic Warfare Officer
FCS	Fire Control System
FEAF	Far East Air Forces
FEW	Fighter-Escort Wing
FEWSG	Fleet Electronic Warfare Support Group
Ft	Feet
Ft/Min	Feet per Minute
FTW	Flying Training Wing
HF	High Frequency
IAS	Indicated Air Speed
ICBM	Intercontinental Ballistic Missile
IRBM	Intermediate Range Ballistic Missile
Km/h	Kilometres per hour
Km	Kilometres
LABS	Low Altitude Bombing System
MAC	Military Airlift Command
MASDC	Military Aircraft Storage and Disposition Center
MATS	Military Air Transport Service
MITO	Minimum Interval Take-Off
mm	Millimetres
MPH	Miles per hour
NACA	National Advisory Committee for Aeronautics
OMS	Organizational Maintenance Squadron
PACCS	Post Attack Command and Control System
PACCS	Post Attack Command Control Squadron
RAF	Royal Air Force
RATO	Rocket Assisted Take-Off
RBS	Radar Bomb Scoring
RCAF	Royal Canadian Air Force
RDT&E	Research, Development, Test and Evaluation
RS(VLR, Photo-RCM)	Reconnaissance Squadron (Very Long Range, Photographic-Radio Countermeasures)
SAC	Strategic Air Command
SAW	Strategic Aerospace Wing
SLAR	Side-Looking Airborne Radar
SRS	Strategic Reconnaissance Squadron
SRS(M)	Strategic Reconnaissance Squadron (Medium)
SRW	Strategic Reconnaissance Wing
SRW(M)	Strategic Reconnaissance Wing (Medium)
SS	Support Squadron
SW	Strategic Wing
TDY	Temporary Duty
UHF	Ultra High Frequency
UK	United Kingdom
USAF	United States Air Force
USAAF	United States Army Air Force
VHF	Very High Frequency
WRS	Weather Reconnaissance Squadron

Specifications

B-47E Model

Type: Strategic Bomber

Number of Crew: Three, comprising pilot, copilot/gunner and bombardier/navigator.

Powerplant: Six General Electric J47-GE-25A turbojet engines, each rated at 6,000 lb st (2722 kg) dry and 7,200 lb st (3266 kg) with water methanol injection. Additional thrust for takeoff in emergency provided by 20 or 30 1,000 lb (454 kg) thrust RATO bottles on jettisonable unit located beneath aft fuselage.

Armament: Two M-24A1 20-mm cannon with 350 rounds of ammunition each in radar-directed tail barbette. Maximum 20,000 lb (9072 kg) bomb-load in internal weapons bay, including four B28 nuclear bombs or conventional general-purpose weapons.

Performance: Maximum speed 606 mph (975 km/h) (Mach 0.84) at 16,300 ft (4968 m); 557 mph (896 km/h) (Mach 0.842) at 38,550 ft (11,750 m); maximum cruise speed 495 mph (797 km/h) (Mach 0.75) at 38,550 ft (11,750 m); initial climb rate at 160,000 lb (72,574 kg) gross weight 4,660 ft/min (1420 m/min); initial climb rate at 206,700 lb (93,757 kg) gross weight 2,300 ft/min (701 m/min); service ceiling 40,500 ft (12,344 m); unrefuelled range with 10,000 lb (4536 kg) weapons load 4,000 miles (6437 km).

Weights: Empty 80,756 lb (36,630 kg); normal loaded 206,700 lb (93,757 kg); maximum overload 220,000 lb (99,790 kg).

Dimensions: Wing span 116 ft 0 in (35.36 m); length 107 ft 0 in (32.61 m); height 27 ft 11 in (8.51 m); wing area 1,428 sq ft (132.66 m^2).

Appendices

Appendix 1: **B-47 Production Details**

Boeing (Wichita)

Variant	Serial No.	Construction No.	Quantity
B-47A-BW	49-1900/909	450001/010	10
B-47B-1-BW	49-2642/645	450011/014	4
B-47B-5-BW	49-2646	450015	1
B-47B-5-BW	50-001/012	450016/027	12
B-47B-10-BW	50-013/025	450028/040	13
B-47B-15-BW	50-026/050	450041/065	25
B-47B-20-BW	50-051/082	450066/097	32
B-47B-25-BW	51-2045/081	450098/134	37
B-47B-30-BW	51-2082/136	450135/189	55
B-47B-35-BW	51-2137/191	450190/244	55
B-47B-40-BW	51-2192/246	450245/299	55
B-47B-45-BW	51-2247/301	450300/354	55
B-47B-50-BW	51-2302/356	450355/409	55
B-47E-55-BW	51-2357/411	450410/464	55
B-47E-60-BW	51-2412/445	450465/498	34
B-47E-60-BW	51-5214/234	450499/519	21
B-47E-65-BW	51-5235/257	450520/542	23
RB-47E-1-BW	51-5258/264	450543/549	7
RB-47E-5-BW	51-5265/270	450550/555	6
RB-47E-10-BW	51-5271/276	450556/561	6
B-47E-65-BW	51-7019/050	450562/593	32
B-47E-70-BW	51-7051/064	450594/607	14
B-47E-75-BW	51-7065/083	450608/626	19
RB-47E-10-BW	51-15821/827	450627/633	7
RB-47E-15-BW	51-15828/853	450634/659	26
B-47E-75-BW	51-17368/386	450660/678	19
B-47E-80-BW	52-394/431	450679/716	38
B-47E-85-BW	52-432/469	450717/754	38
B-47E-90-BW	52-470/507	450755/792	38
B-47E-95-BW	52-508/545	450793/830	38
B-47E-100-BW	52-546/583	450831/868	38
B-47E-105-BW	52-584/620	450869/905	37
RB-47E-20-BW	52-685/719	450906/940	35
RB-47E-25-BW	52-720/754	450941/975	35
RB-47E-30-BW	52-755/789	450976/1010	35
RB-47E-35-BW	52-790/825	4501011/046	36
RB-47E-40-BW	52-3374/400	4501047/073	27
B-47E-110-BW	53-2261/296	4501074/109	36

B-47E-115-BW	53-2297/331	4501110/144	35
B-47E-120-BW	53-2332/367	4501145/180	36
B-47E-125-BW	53-2368/402	4501181/215	35
B-47E-130-BW	53-2403/417	4501216/230	15
B-47E-130-BW	53-4207/244	4501231/268	38
RB-47E-45-BW	53-4245/264	4501269/288	20
RB-47K-1-BW	53-4265/279	4501289/303	15
RB-47H-1-BW	53-4280/309	4501304/333	30
B-47E-135-BW	53-6193/244	4501334/385	52
RB-47H-1-BW	53-6245/249	4501386/390	5

Douglas (Tulsa)

Variant	Serial No.	Construction No.	Quantity
B-47E-1-DT	52-019/028	43634/643	10
B-47E-5-DT	52-029/041	43644/656	13
B-47E-10-DT	52-042/054	43657/669	13
B-47E-10-DT	52-055/058	43751/754	4
B-47E-15-DT	52-059/081	43755/777	23
B-47E-20-DT	52-082/111	43778/807	30
B-47E-25-DT	52-112/120	43808/816	9
B-47E-25-DT	52-146/176	44000/030	31
B-47E-30-DT	52-177/201	44031/055	25
B-47E-35-DT	52-1406/417	44090/101	12
B-47E-35-DT	53-2028/040	44149/161	13
B-47E-40-DT	53-2090/103	44436/449	14
B-47E-45-DT	53-2104/117	44450/463	14
B-47E-50-DT	53-2118/131	44464/477	14
B-47E-55-DT	53-2132/144	44478/490	13
B-47E-60-DT	53-2145/157	44491/503	13
B-47E-65-DT	53-2158/170	44504/516	13

Douglas (Tulsa) also assembled B-47Bs: 51-2141, 51-2150, 51-2155, 51-2160, 51-2165, 51-2170, 51-2175, 51-2180, 51-2185 and 51-2190, allocating construction numbers 43624 to 43633 to these 10 aircraft, all of which were originally manufactured by Boeing at its Wichita facility.

Lockheed (Marietta)

Variant	Serial No.	Construction No.	Quantity
B-47E-5-LM	51-15804/810	1/7	7
B-47E-10-LM	51-15811/812	8/9	2
B-47E-10-LM	52-202/207	10/15	6
B-47E-15-LM	52-208/220	16/28	13
B-47E-20-LM	52-221/235	29/43	15
B-47E-25-LM	52-236/260	44/68	25
B-47E-30-LM	52-261/292	69/100	32
B-47E-35-LM	52-293/330	101/138	38
B-47E-40-LM	52-331/362	139/170	32
B-47E-45-LM	52-363/393	171/201	31
B-47E-50-LM	52-3343/373	202/232	31
B-47E-55-LM	53-1819/849	233/263	31
B-47E-60-LM	53-1850/880	264/294	31
B-47E-65-LM	53-1881/911	295/325	31
B-47E-70-LM	53-1912/942	326/356	31
B-47E-75-LM	53-1943/972	357/386	30

Lockheed (Marietta) also assembled B-47Bs: 51-2145, 51-2197, 51-2204, 51-2210, 51-2217, 51-2224, 51-2231, 51-2237 and 51-2243, all of these nine aircraft originally being manufactured by Boeing at its Wichita facility. No separate construction numbers were allocated to these Stratojets.

Boeing (Seattle)

Variant	Serial No.	Construction No.	Quantity
XB-47-BO	46-065/066	15972/973	2

Production Breakdown by Variant

Variant	Serial No.	Batch Total	Type Total
XB-47	46-065/066	2	2
B-47A	49-1900/909	10	10
B-47B	49-2642/646	5	
	50-001/082	82	
	51-2045/356	312	399
B-47E	51-2357/445	89	
	51-5214/257	44	
	51-7019/083	65	
	51-15804/812	9	
	51-17368/386	19	
	52-019/120	102	
	52-146/620	475	
	52-1406/417	12	
	52-3343/373	31	
	53-1819/972	154	
	53-2028/040	13	
	53-2090/170	81	
	53-2261/417	157	
	53-4207/244	38	
	53-6193/244	52	1,341
RB-47E	51-5258/276	19	
	51-15821/853	33	
	52-685/825	141	
	52-3374/400	27	
	53-4245/264	20	240
RB-47H	53-4280/309	30	
	53-6245/249	5	35
RB-47K	53-4265/279	15	15

Total = 2,042

Appendix 2: **B-47 Variants**

XB-47	New-build—2 produced
B-47A	New-build—10 produced
B-47B	New-build—399 produced
B-47E	New-build—1,341 produced
RB-47E	New-build—240 produced
RB-47H	New-build—35 produced
RB-47K	New-build—15 produced

B-47B-II   Resulted from modification programme initiated in late 1954 which brought basic B-47B model to standard approaching that of B-47E.

DB-47B   Unarmed drone director. Converted from B-47B. Some sources say 74 aircraft involved whilst others refer to only four. Almost certainly allied to Bell GAM-63 Rascal air-to-surface guided missile.

TB-47B   66 B-47Bs modified for crew training. Featured fourth seat for instructor. Unarmed.

WB-47B   One aircraft converted for weather reconnaissance with 55th WRS of MATS AWS. In service from 11/57 until 1963.

YRB-47B   Total of 91 aircraft converted from standard B-47B to take eight-camera reconnaissance pack in bomb bay. Has also been referred to as RB-47B. Mainly employed as trainer for RB-47E production model. In service from 1953 until 1955.

B-47C   Proposed production model with J71 engine.

RB-47C   Proposed production model with J71 engine.

YB-47C   Single B-47B earmarked for modification to take four YJ71-A-5 engines plus provision for reconnaissance pack. Originally designated XB-56. Not proceeded with.

XB-47D   Two B-47Bs modified to serve as engine test-beds with mixed propulsion, comprising two J47-GE-23 turbojets outboard and two Wright YT49-W-1 turboprops inboard.

B-47E-II   Updated B-47E for low-level penetration incorporating structural strengthening as part of Project Milk Bottle.

B-47E-IV   Updated B-47E incorporating structural strengthening.

DB-47E   Two aircraft modified to serve as drone directors.

EB-47E   ECM-configured aircraft with removable bomb-bay sensor package.

EB-47E (TT)   Three aircraft modified to take bomb-bay capsule containing two EWOs. Used to monitor Soviet space shots and IRBM testing.

ETB-47E   Unspecified number of B-47Es modified to undertake electronics crew training duties.

JB-47E   Temporary test designation applied to small number of B-47Es.

JQB-47E   Temporary test designation applied to at least one drone-configured QB-47E aircraft.

JRB-47E   Designation applied to at least one RB-47E modified to undertake temporary test duties.

NB-47E   Designation applied to unspecified number of aircraft assigned to permanent test duties.

QB-47E   14 RB-47E modified as radio-controlled drone targets for use by 3205th Drone Group. Featured arrester hook behind rear mainwheels plus pods with control/telemetry equipment.

WB-47E   34 B-47Es modified for weather reconnaissance tasks with MATS AWS. Last examples retired in 1970.

YDB-47E   Two aircraft modified to carry GAM-63 Rascal.

YB-47F   One B-47B modified with probe to take part in in-flight refuelling tests.

KB-47G   One B-47B modified to take bomb bay-mounted hose and reel in-flight refuelling equipment. Took part in test project with YB-47F.

ERB-47H   Three RB-47Hs modified for electronic mission of unspecified nature. Five man crew.

YB-47J   Single B-47E modified to test MA.2 radar bombing and navigation attack system.

EB-47L   35 B-47Es modified as radio relay platforms to form part of post-attack command and control system. Replaced by EC-135.

RB-56A   Reconnaissance project which was abandoned. See YB-47C and XB-56/YB-56.

XB-56/ YB-56   Proposal for four-engined aircraft utilizing YJ71-A-5 turbojets. Plans to modify B-47B implemented, this being given new designation YB-47C. Cancelled before reaching flight test stage. See YB-47C.

CL-52   One B-47B bailed to Canadair for use as engine test bed with single 20,000 lb st (9072 kg) Orenda Iroquois turbojet engine in pod attached to starboard aft fuselage. Known by company as CL-52, this acquired full RCAF insignia.

Appendix 3: **SAC B-47 Major Bases**

CONTINENTAL USA

Abilene, Tx	96 BW (9/57-3/63); 341 BW (55-6/61)
Altus, Ok	96 BW (6/55-9/57)
Barksdale, La	301 BW (7/53-4/58); 376 BW (2/54-12/57)
Biggs, Tx★	97 BW (7/55-1/59)
Bunker Hill, In	305 BW (6/59-61)
Castle, Ca	93 BW (5/54-56)
Chennault, La★	(base formerly known as Lake Charles AFB, La)
Davis-Monthan, Az	43 BW (1/54-3/60); 303 BW (3/53-6/64)
Dyess, Tx	(base formerly known as Abilene AFB, Tx)
Forbes, Ks★	40 BW (6/60-8/64); 55 SRW (9/54-8/66); 90 SRW (6/54-6/60)
Homestead, Fl	19 BW (6/56-7/61); 379 BW (4/56-60)
Hunter, Ga★	2 BW (2/54-4/63); 308 BW (1/54-7/59)
Lake Charles, La ★	44 BW (6/53-6/60); 68 BW (10/53-3/63)
Lincoln, Ne★	98 BW (12/54-12/65); 307 BW (3/55-3/65); 4362 SS (8/62-12/64)
Little Rock, Ar	384 BW (2/56-8/64); 70 SRW/BW (55-6/62)
Lockbourne, Oh	301 BW (4/58-6/64); 376 BW (12/57-3/65); 26 SRW (9/53-4/58); 91 SRW (5/53-11/57); 4363 SS (11/62-3/65)
MacDill, Fl	305 BW (52-6/59); 306 BW (10/51-4/63)
March, Ca	22 BW (1/53-3/63); 320 BW (7/53-9/60)
McConnell, Ks	4347 CCTW (7/58-6/63)
McCoy, Fl★	(base formerly known as Pinecastle AFB, Fl)
Mountain Home, Id	9 BW (9/54-2/66); 4364 SS (12/62-3/65)
Offutt, Ne	55 SRW (8/66-12/67)
Pease, NH	(base formerly known as Portsmouth AFB, NH)
Pinecastle, Fl★	19 BW (10/54-6/56); 321 BW (5/54-9/61)
Plattsburgh, NY	380 BW (12/55-12/65); 4365 SS (7/62-9/64); 308 BW (7/59-6/61 not equipped or manned)
Portsmouth, NH	100 BW (1/56-2/66); 509 BW (7/58-11/65)
Roswell, NM★	509 BW (6/55-7/58)
Schilling, Ks★	(base formerly known as Smoky Hill AFB, Ks)
Sedalia, Mo	340 BW (4/54-63)
Smoky Hill, Ks★	40 BW (8/54-6/60); 310 BW (6/54-2/65)
Walker, NM★	(base formerly known as Roswell AFB, NM)
Whiteman, Mo	(base formerly known as Sedalia AFB, Mo)

★Now closed.

OVERSEAS

FRENCH MOROCCO—B-47 operations from bases in French Morocco are understood to have begun during 1954. The three airfields listed all supported SAC's Stratojet force at various times until July 1963 when 'Reflex Action' simultaneously ceased at all three, this method of B-47 deployment having originally begun at Sidi Slimane during July 1957 on a trial basis.

Ben Guerir, Nouasseur and Sidi Slimane

SPAIN—B-47 operations in Spain got under way during July 1957 when 15 aircraft of the 40th BW moved from Greenham Common to Zaragoza for a short exercise. 'Reflex Action' began here soon afterwards, continuing at Zaragoza until April 1964 and at Moron and Torrejon until the end of March 1965.

Moron, Torrejon and Zaragoza

GUAM—This, the sole base on Guam, hosted SAC bomber operations (including B-47s) for many years. Following a change in methods of deployment during the latter half of the fifties, an operation code-named 'Air Mail' began, this being similar to 'Reflex Action' and involving B-47s. The Stratojet continued to conduct 'Air Mail' activities until April 1964 when it gave way to the larger B-52, a type which still operates from Andersen today.

Andersen

ALASKA—Rotational and 'Reflex Action' operations with the B-47 were conducted from these Alaskan bases for many years, activities of this nature finally terminating in 1965.

Eielson and Elmendorf

GREAT BRITAIN—No less than eight bases in Great Britain supported B-47 operations during the fifties and sixties. Fairford was the first overseas base to be visited by a B-47 wing engaged in the 60/90-day rotational training programme, other airfields which hosted units on a temporary basis being Brize Norton, Upper Heyford, Greenham Common and Lakenheath. 'Reflex Action' was initiated in the UK at Fairford and Greenham Common on 7 January 1958 and at its peak—in the first six months of 1959—no less than seven bases were involved, these being Brize Norton, Upper Heyford, Greenham Common, Fairford, Mildenhall, Chelveston and Bruntingthorpe. 'Reflex Action' ceased at the latter three locations in the summer of 1959, continuing at Fairford and Greenham Common until the end of May 1964 and at Brize Norton and Upper Heyford until the end of March 1965, the last B-47s returning to Pease AFB, New Hampshire (509 BW from Upper Heyford) and Plattsburgh AFB, New York (380 SAW from Brize Norton) in early April 1965.

Brize Norton, Bruntingthorpe, Chelveston, Fairford, Greenham Common, Lakenheath, Mildenhall and Upper Heyford

Appendix 4: **SAC B-47 Operating Units 1951–67**

Bomb Wings (Medium)

No.	Period	Prime Sqdns.	Alert Sqdn.
2 BW	2/54-4/63	20/49/96 BS	429 BS
9 BW	9/54-2/66	1/5/99 BS	658 BS
19 BW	10/54-7/61	28/30/93 BS	659 BS
22 BW	1/53-3/63	2/19/33 BS	408 BS
40 BW	8/54-8/64	25/44/45 BS	660 BS
43 BW	1/54-3/60	63/64/65 BW	403 BS
44 BW	6/53-6/60	66/67/68 BW	506 BS
68 BW	10/53-3/63	51/52/656 BS	657 BS
70 BW	10/61-6/62	6/61/681 BS	—
93 BW	5/54-56	328/329/330 BS	—
96 BW	6/55-3/63	337/338/339 BS	413 BS
97 BW	7/55-1/59	340/341/342 BS	—
98 BW	12/54-12/65	343/344/345 BS	415 BS
100 BW	1/56-2/66	349/350/351 BS	418 BS
301 BW	7/53-6/64	32/352/353 BS	419 BS
303 BW	3/53-6/64	358/359/360 BS	427 BS
305 BW	52-61	364/365/366 BS	422 BS
306 BW	10/51-4/63	367/368/369 BS	423 BS
307 BW	3/55-3/65	370/371/372 BS	424 BS
308 BW	1/54-7/59	373/374/375 BS	425 BS
310 BW	6/54-2/65	379/380/381 BS	428 BS
320 BW	7/53-9/60	441/442/443 BS	444 BS
321 BW	5/54-9/61	445/446/447 BS	448 BS
340 BW	4/54-9/63	486/487/488 BS	489 BS
341 BW	55-6/61	10/12/490 BS	491 BS
376 BW	2/54-3/65	512/513/514 BS	515 BS
379 BW	4/56-60	524/525/526 BS	527 BS
380 BW	12/55-12/65	528/529/530 BS	531 BS
384 BW	2/56-8/64	544/545/546 BS	547 BS
509 BW	6/55-11/65	393/715/830 BS	661 BS

Note: 70th BW was formerly the 70th SRW, being redesignated on 25/10/61.

Strategic Reconnaissance Wings (Medium)

No.	Period	Sqdns.
26 SRW	9/53-4/58	3/4/10 SRS
55 SRW	9/54-12/67	38/338/343 SRS
70 SRW	55-10/61	6/26/61 SRS (see note)
90 SRW	6/54-6/60	319/320/321 SRS
91 SRW	5/53-11/57	322/323/324 SRS

Note: 70 SRW was redesignated as 70 BW on 25/10/61, the 26 SRS being simultaneously renumbered the 681 BS while the 6 SRS and 61 SRS became the 6 BS and 61 BS respectively.

Combat Crew Training Wing

No.	Period	Sqdns.
4347 CCTW	7/58-6/63	4347/4348/4349/4350 CCTS

Support Squadrons/Post-Attack Command and Control Squadrons

No.	Period
4362 SS	8/62-12/64
4363 SS	11/62-3/65
4364 SS	12/62-3/65
4365 SS	7/62-9/64

Note: All four Support Squadrons were redesignated as Post-Attack Command and Control Squadrons during 1964.

Appendix 5: **SAC B-47 Wings and Squadrons**

2 BW(M) Converted from B-50 to B-47 at Hunter AFB, Georgia in 2/54, retaining this type until 1/4/63 when redesignated as 2 BW(H) and simultaneously relocated to Barksdale AFB, Louisiana with the B-52F. Was a 'superstrength' Wing with 70 aircraft between 7/59 and 4/61.

20 BS(M) Utilized B-47 from 1954 until 1/4/63 when redesignated 20 BS(H) on moving to Barksdale where it received personnel and aircraft previously assigned to the 4238 SW.

49 BS(M) Utilized B-47 from 1954 until 1/4/63 when discontinued.

96 BS(M) Utilized B-47 from 1954 until 1/4/63 when discontinued.

429 BS Redesignated from 429 BS(H) to 429 BS(M) on 11/8/58 and activated 1/10/58 to support 2 BW alert commitment. Not operational from 6/11/61 until 1/1/62 when discontinued and inactivated. Equipped with B-47 from 10/58 until 11/61.

9 BW(M) Converted from B-29 to B-47 at Mountain Home AFB, Idaho in 9/54, retaining this type until 11/2/66 when last example (36235) was retired. Redesignated as 9 SAW on 1/4/62. Remained active in non-operational status until 25/6/66 when redesignated as 9 SRW and relocated to Beale AFB, California, inheriting SR-71 aircraft and personnel previously assigned to the 4200th SRW at the same base.

1 BS(M) Utilized B-47 from 1954 until 2/66. Redesignated 1 SRS on 25/6/66, taking over assets from 4201 SRS.

5 BS(M) Utilized B-47 from 1954 until 2/66. Discontinued on 25/6/66.

99 BS(M) Utilized B-47 from 1954 until 2/66. Redesignated 99 SRS on 25/6/66 to operate SR-71.

658 BS(M) Activated 1/10/58 to support 9 BW alert commitment. Not operational from 1/10/61 until discontinued and inactivated on 1/1/62. Equipped with B-47 from 10/58 until 10/61.

4364 SS Organized at Mountain Home AFB, Idaho with the EB-47L as part of 9 SAW on 20/7/62, but did not become operational until circa 1/12/62. Redesignated 4364 PACCS during 1964, subsequently being inactivated on 25/3/65.

19 BW(M) Equipped with B-47 at Pinecastle AFB, Florida in 10/54 and relocated to Homestead AFB, Florida on 1/6/56. Retained B-47 until 1/7/61 when redesignated as 19 BW(H) to operate the B-52H Stratofortress from the same base.

28 BS(M) Utilized B-47 from 10/54 until 1/7/61. Redesignated 28 BS(H) on that date and equipped with the B-52H during 1962.

30 BS(M) Utilized B-47 from 10/54 until 1/7/61. Redesignated 30 BS(H) on that date and subsequently reassigned to 4133 SW at Grand Forks AFB, North Dakota on 1/1/62, receiving B-52H in 1962.

93 BS(M) Utilized B-47 from 10/54 until 1/7/61. Redesignated 93 BS(H) on that date and subsequently reassigned to 4239 SW at Kincheloe AFB, Michigan on 1/8/61, receiving B-52H in November of the same year.

659 BS(M) Activated on 1/11/58 to support 19 BW alert commitment. Discontinued and inactivated on 1/7/61. Used B-47 from 11/58 until 7/61.

22 BW(M) Converted from B-29 to B-47 at March AFB, California in 1/53, retaining this type until 15/3/63 when redesignated as the 22 BW(H) which was earmarked to operate the B-52B Stratofortress from the same base.

2 BS(M) Utilized B-47 from 1/53 until 3/63. Discontinued on 15/3/63 but redesignated 2 BS(H) and reassigned to 22 BW(H) on 15/9/63 with B-52B.

19 BS(M) Utilized B-47 from 1/53 until discontinued and inactivated on 15/3/63.

33 BS(M) Utilized B-47 from 1/53 until discontinued and inactivated on 15/3/63.

408 BS Redesignated from 408 BS(H) to 408 BS(M) on 6/10/58 and activated on 1/1/59 to support 22 BW alert commitment. Not operational from 21/10/61 until 1/1/62 when discontinued and inactivated. Equipped with B-47 from 1/59 until 10/61.

26 SRW(M) Established on 9/5/52 as 26 SRW(M) and activated at Lockbourne AFB, Ohio on 28/5/52 although not manned until 1/53. Received RB-47 during 1953, retaining this type until 4/58. Inactivated 1/7/58.

3 SRS Reconstituted and redesignated 3 SRS(M) on 9/5/52 and activated on 28/5/52. Not operational from 28/5/52 until 1/3/53 and from 15/4/58 until inactivated on 1/7/58. Equipped with YRB-47 in 1953-54, RB-47 in 1954-58 and B-47 in 1958.

4 SRS Redesignated 4 SRS(M) on 9/5/52 and activated on 28/5/52. Not operational from 28/5/52 until 2/9/53 and from 15/4/58 until inactivated on 1/7/58. Equipped with YRB/RB/B-47 during 1953-58.

10 SRS Redesignated 10 SRS(M) on 9/5/52 and activated on 28/5/52. Not operational from 28/5/52 until circa 1/10/53 and from 15/4/58 until inactivated on 1/7/58. Equipped with YRB-47 in 1954 and RB-47 in 1954-58.

40 BW(M) Converted from B-29 to B-47 at Smoky Hill AFB, Kansas in 8/54, retaining this type until 8/64. Relocated to Forbes AFB, Kansas on 20/6/60 and redesignated 40 SAW on 1/2/64. Discontinued and inactivated on 1/9/64.

25 BS(M) Utilized B-47 from 8/54 until 8/64, being discontinued and inactivated on 1/9/64.

44 BS(M) Utilized B-47 from 8/54 until 8/64, being discontinued and inactivated on 1/9/64.

45 BS(M) Utilized B-47 from 8/54 until 8/64, being discontinued and inactivated on 1/9/64.

660 BS(M) Activated on 1/2/59 to support 40 BW alert commitment. Discontinued and inactivated on 1/1/62 but was probably not operational from circa 10/61 onwards. Utilized B-47 from 2/59 until 10/61.

43 BW(M) Converted from B-50 to B-47 in 1/54 at Davis-Monthan AFB, Arizona. Operated B-47 until 15/3/60 when relocated to Carswell AFB, Texas and re-equipped with B-58A Hustler.

63 BS(M) Utilized B-47 from 1/54 until 15/3/60.

64 BS(M) Utilized B-47 from 1/54 until 15/3/60.

65 BS(M) Utilized B-47 from 1/54 until 15/3/60.

403 BS Redesignated from 403 BS(H) to 403 BS(M) on 20/8/58 and activated 1/12/58 to support 43 BW alert commitment. Discontinued on 15/3/60, coincident with move of parent wing from Davis-Monthan to Carswell. Utilized B-47 from 1958 until 15/3/60.

44 BW(M) Converted from B-29 to B-47 at Lake Charles AFB, Louisiana in June 1953. Used B-47 until 15/6/60 when unit discontinued.

66 BS(M) Utilized B-47 from 6/53 until discontinued on 15/6/60.

67 BS(M) Utilized B-47 from 6/53 until discontinued on 15/6/60.

68 BS(M) Utilized B-47 from 6/53 until discontinued on 15/6/60.

506 BS Redesignated from 506 BS(VH) to 506 BS(M) on 20/8/58 and activated 1/12/58 to support 44 BW alert commitment. Discontinued on 15/6/60. Equipped with B-47 from 1958 until 15/6/60.

55 SRW(M) Converted from RB-50 to RB-47 at Forbes AFB, Kansas in 9/54. Relocated from Forbes to Offutt AFB, Nebraska on 16/8/66 and simultaneously redesignated as 55 SRW. Continued to operate the RB-47 until 12/67 when last aircraft retired by 338 SRS.

38 SRS(M) Received RB-47E in 9/54, retaining this model until converted to RB-47H in 1955–56. Retained RB-47H until 1965 when relocated to Offutt AFB, Nebraska for 'Looking Glass' airborne command post duties with EC-135.

338 SRS(M) Received RB-47E in 9/54, retaining this model until converted to RB-47K circa 1955–56. Retained RB-47K on weather reconnaissance tasks until inactivated on 15/6/60. Reactivated at Offutt on 25/3/67 to operate remaining examples of the RB-47H. Inactivated 25/12/67 shortly before last RB-47H was retired to storage at MASDC at Davis-Monthan AFB, Arizona. Was last SAC element to operate the Stratojet.

343 SRS(M) Received RB-47E in 9/54, retaining this model until converted to RB-47H in 1955–56. Retained RB-47H until circa 25/3/67 when turned over remaining aircraft to 338 SRS so as to concentrate on converting to the RC-135C, the first example of which was delivered to the 343 SRS on 27/1/67.

68 BW(M) Converted from B-29 to B-47 at Lake Charles AFB, Louisiana in October 1953. B-47 retained until 20/3/63 when last example retired. Identity transferred to Seymour-Johnson AFB, North Carolina on 15/4/63 as 68 BW(H) with B-52G.

51 BS(M) Utilized B-47 from 10/53 until 3/63. Redesignated 51 BS(H) on 15/4/63 and relocated to Seymour-Johnson with B-52G as part of 68 BW(H).

52 BS(M) Utilized B-47 from 10/53 until 3/63. Discontinued 15/4/63.

656 BS(M) Utilized B-47 from 10/53 until 3/63. Discontinued 15/4/63.

657 BS(M) Activated on 1/12/58 to support 68 BW(M) alert commitment. Not operational from 1/10/61 until 1/1/62 when discontinued and inactivated. Utilized B-47 12/58 until 10/61.

70 SRW(M) Established as 70 SRW(M) on 22/3/53 and activated at Little Rock AFB, Arkansas on 24/1/55 to operate RB-47. Redesignated 70 BW(M) on 25/10/61 but inactivated 25/6/62. Was employed on combat crew training tasks between 6/58 and 9/61. Converted to B-47 in late 1961 but inactivated before becoming combat ready.

6 SRS Redesignated from 6 RS(VLR, Photo-RCM) to 6 SRS(M) on 14/1/55 and activated 24/1/55 to operate RB-47. Redesignated 6 BS(M) on 25/10/61. Discontinued and inactivated on 25/6/62. Utilized RB-47 from 1955 until 1962 and B-47 during 1961–62.

26 SRS Redesignated from 26 RS(VLR, Photo-RCM) to 26 SRS(M) on 14/1/55 and activated 24/1/55 to operate RB-47. Redesignated 681 BS(M) on 25/10/61. Utilized RB-47 from 1955 until 1961.

61 SRS(M) Activated 24/1/55 to operate RB-47. Redesignated 61 BS(M) on 25/10/61. Discontinued and inactivated on 25/6/62. Utilised RB-47 from 1955 until 1962 and B-47 during 1961–62.

681 BS(M) Created on 25/10/61 through redesignation of 26 SRS(M). Discontinued and inactivated on 25/6/62. Equipped with RB-47 and B-47 during 1961–62.

90 SRW(M) Converted from B/RB-29 to RB-47 at Forbes AFB, Kansas in 6/54, retaining this type until discontinued on 20/6/60. Served as combat crew training unit from 5/58 until discontinued.

319 SRS(M) Utilized RB-47 from 1954 until discontinued on 20/6/60.

320 SRS(M) Utilized RB-47 from 1954 until discontinued on 20/6/60.

321 SRS(M) Utilized RB-47 from 1954 until discontinued on 20/6/60.

91 SRW(M) Converted from B/RB-45 to RB-47 at Lockbourne AFB, Ohio in 5/53, retaining this type until inactivated on 8/11/57. Also operated B-47 in 1953 and YRB-47 in 1953–54.

322 SRS(M) Utilized B/RB/YRB-47 from 1953 until inactivated on 8/11/57.

323 SRS(M) Utilized B/RB/YRB-47 from 1953 until inactivated on 8/11/57.

324 SRS(M) Utilized B/RB/YRB-47 from 1953 until inactivated on 8/11/57.

93 BW(M) Converted from B-50 to B-47 at Castle AFB, California in 5/54, retaining some examples of this type until 1956 and latterly operating them on crew training tasks alongside B-52s. Redesignated as 93 BW(H) on 1/2/55 in anticipation of receiving first B-52B in 6/55.

328 BS(M) Utilized B-47 during 1954–56, being redesignated as 328 BS(H) on 1/2/55.

329 BS(M) Utilized B-47 during 1954–56, being redesignated as 329 BS(H) on 1/2/55.

330 BS(M) Utilized B-47 during 1954–56, being redesignated as 330 BS(H) on 1/2/55.

96 BW(M) Redesignated 96 BW(M) on 6/11/53 and activated at Altus AFB, Oklahoma on 18/11/53 but was not equipped with B-47 until 6/55 onward. Moved to Dyess AFB, Texas on 8/9/57 and continued to operate B-47 from there until 15/3/63. Redesignated 96 SAW on 1/4/62. Began operations with B-52E in 12/63.

337 BS Redesignated from 337 BS(VH) to 337 BS(M) on 6/11/53 and activated on 18/11/53. Not operational between 18/11/53 and 13/3/55. Equipped with B-47 from 1955 until 15/3/63 when discontinued. Reorganised 15/9/63 as 337 BS(H) for B-52.

338 BS Redesignated from 338 BS(VH) to 338 BS(M) on 6/11/53 and activated on 18/11/53. Not operational between 18/11/53 and 13/3/55. Discontinued 15/3/63. Equipped with B-47 from 1955 until 1963.

339 BS Redesignated from 339 BS(VH) to 339 BS(M) on 6/11/53 and activated on 18/11/53. Not operational between 18/11/53 and 29/4/55. Discontinued 15/3/63. Equipped with B-47 from 1955 until 1963.

413 BS Redesignated from 413 BS(VH) to 413 BS(M) on 20/8/58 and activated on 1/11/58 to support 96 BW alert commitment. Not operational from 1/10/61 until 1/1/62. Discontinued and inactivated on 1/1/62. Equipped with B-47 from 1958 to 1961.

97 BW(M) Converted from B-50 to B-47 in 7/55 at Biggs AFB, Texas. Operated B-47 until 1/59, subsequently moving without men or equipment to Blytheville AFB, Arkansas on 1/7/59 where it was redesignated as the 97 BW(H) on 1/10/59 and equipped with B-52G.

340 BS(M) Operated B-47 from 1955 until 1959. Redesignated 340 BS(H) on 1/10/59 and received B-52G as part of 97 BW(H) in 1/60.

341 BS(M) Operated B-47 from 1955 until 1959. Redesignated 341 BS(H) on 1/10/59 and reassigned to Dow AFB, Maine on 15/2/60 to operate the B-52G as part of the 4038 SW.

342 BS(M) Operated B-47 from 1955 until 1959. Redesignated 342 BS(H) on 1/10/59 and reassigned to Robins AFB, Georgia on 1/5/60 to operate the B-52G as part of the 4137 SW.

98 BW(M) Equipped with B-47 at Lincoln AFB, Nebraska in 12/54 and continued to operate this type until 12/65, being redesignated 98 SAW on 1/2/64. Remained in existence in non-operational state until 25/6/66 when discontinued and inactivated.

343 BS(M) Utilized B-47 from 1954 until 12/65. Non-operational from 12/65 until discontinued and inactivated on 25/6/66.

344 BS(M) Utilized B-47 from 1954 until 12/65. Non-operational from 12/65 until discontinued and inactivated on 25/6/66.

345 BS(M) Utilized B-47 from 1954 until 12/65. Non-operational from 12/65 until discontinued and inactivated on 25/6/66.

415 BS Redesignated from 415 BS(H) to 415 BS(M) on 11/8/58 and activated on 1/9/58 to support 98 BW alert commitment. Non-operational from 1/10/61 until discontinued and inactivated on 1/6/62. Utilized B-47 from 1958 and 1961.

100 BW(M) Established as 100 BW(M) at Portsmouth AFB, New Hampshire on 23/3/53 and activated 1/1/56. Operated B-47 from 1956 until 11/2/66 when last aircraft (32286) was retired. Remained in existence in non-operational status until 25/6/66 when redesignated as 100 SRW and relocated to Davis-Monthan AFB, Arizona where it inherited aircraft and personnel previously assigned to the 4080 SW.

349 BS Redesignated from 349 BS(VH) to 349 BS(M) on 1/8/55 and activated on 1/1/56. Equipped with B-47 from 1956 until 2/66. Not operational from 12/2/66 until 24/6/66. Redesignated as 349 SRS on 25/6/66 and subsequently operated U-2C/R.

350 BS Redesignated from 350 BS(VH) to 350 BS(M) on 1/8/55 and activated on 1/1/56. Equipped with B-47 from 1956 until 2/66. Not operational from 12/2/66 until 24/6/66. Redesignated as 350 SRS on 25/6/66, subsequently operating DC-130A/E Hercules and assorted drones.

351 BS Redesignated from 351 BS(VH) to 351 BS(M) on 1/8/55 and activated on 1/1/56. Equipped with B-47 from 1956 until 2/66. Not operational from 12/2/66 until 25/6/66 when discontinued and inactivated.

418 BS Redesignated from 418 BS(VH) to 418 BS(M) on 1/12/58 and activated on 1/3/59 to support 100 BW alert commitment. Not operational circa 31/10/61 until 1/1/62 when discontinued and inactivated. Equipped with the B-47 from 1959 to 1961.

301 BW(M) Converted from B-29 to B-47 at Barksdale AFB, Louisiana in 6/53, retaining this type until 6/64. Relocated to Lockbourne AFB, Ohio on 15/4/58. Redesignated 301 ARW 15/6/64 with KC-135A. Primarily concerned with ECM-type missions from 7/58 onwards, employing EB-47E from 1961 until 1964. Some RB-47s also used in 1958 for brief period following change of base.

32 BS(M) Utilized B-47 from 1953 until 8/6/64 when discontinued.

352 BS(M) Utilized B-47 from 1953 until 8/6/64 when discontinued and inactivated.

353 BS(M) Utilized B-47 from 1953 until 8/6/64 when discontinued and inactivated.

419 BS Redesignated from 419 BS(VH) to 419 BS(M) on 20/8/58 and activated on 1/12/58 to support 301 BW alert commitment. Discontinued and inactivated on 1/1/62. Probably not operational from circa 10/61 until discontinued and inactivated. Utilized B-47 between 12/58 and 10/61.

303 BW(M) Converted from B-29 to B-47 at Davis-Monthan AFB, Arizona in 1953. Continued to operate B-47 until discontinued and inactivated on 15/6/64.

358 BS(M) Utilized B-47 from 1953 until discontinued and inactivated on 15/6/64.

359 BS(M) Utilized B-47 from 1953 until discontinued and inactivated on 15/6/64.

360 BS(M) Utilized B-47 from 1953 until discontinued and inactivated on 15/6/64.

427 BS Redesignated from 427 BS(H) to 427 BS(M) on 20/8/58 and activated on 1/12/58 to support 303 BW alert commitment. Not operational between 1/9/61 and 1/1/62 when discontinued and inactivated. Equipped with B-47 from 12/58 until 9/61.

305 BW(M) Established as 305 BW(M) on 20/12/50 and activated at MacDill AFB, Florida on 2/1/51. Controlled activities of 305 BG(M) between 2/1/51 and 16/6/52 when latter was inactivated, having not been operational since 10/2/51. Thereafter, those squadrons previously assigned to the Group and attached to the Wing were assigned directly to the Wing. Converted from B-29 to B-47 in 1952 and retained this type until 1961, having been relocated to Bunker Hill AFB, Indiana on 1/6/59. Re-equipped with B-58 in 1961.

364 BS(M) Utilized B-47 from 1952 until 1961.

365 BS(M) Utilized B-47 from 1952 until 1961.

366 BS(M) Utilized B-47 from 1952 until 1961.

422 BS Redesignated from 422 BS(L) to 422 BS(M) on 6/10/58 and activated on 1/1/59 to support 305 BW alert commitment. Not operational from 1/6/59 until 1/10/59 when reassigned to 3958 Operational Evaluation and Training Group at Carswell AFB, Texas. Reverted to control of the 305 BW on 8/3/60, moving back to Bunker Hill on 15/3/60, but remained in non-operational status until discontinued and inactivated on 15/2/61. Equipped with B-47 between 1/59 and 5/59.

306 BW(M) Established 11/8/48 but not activated at MacDill AFB, Florida until 1/9/50. Controlled 306 BG(M) from 1/9/50 until 16/6/52 although latter was not operational between 10/2/51 and 16/6/52 when it was inactivated. Thereafter, squadrons previously assigned to the Group and attached to the Wing were assigned directly to the Wing. Converted from B-50 to B-47 in late 1951, retaining latter type until early 1963. Was redesignated 306 BW(H) on 1/4/63, moving simultaneously to McCoy AFB, Florida to operate the B-52D.

306 BG(M) Converted from B-50 to B-47 at MacDill AFB, Florida in 10/51 but was non-operational, all three assigned squadrons being attached to the 306 BW for operational control. Inactivated on 16/6/52, squadrons then being directly assigned to the 306 BW(M).

367 BS(M) Converted from B-50 to B-47 in 10/51 and retained latter type until early 1963. Not operational from 3/1/63 until 1/4/63 when moved to McCoy AFB, Florida to operate B-52D, being simultaneously redesignated 367 BS(H).

368 BS(M) Converted from B-50 to B-47 in 10/51 and retained latter type until early 1963. Discontinued and inactivated on 1/4/63.

369 BS(M) Converted from B-50 to B-47 in 10/51 and retained latter type until early 1963. Not operational from 3/1/63 until 1/4/63 when discontinued and inactivated.

423 BS Redesignated from 423 BS(L) to 423 BS(M) on 6/10/58 and activated on 1/1/59 to support 306 BW alert commitment. Not operational from 15/10/61 until discontinued and inactivated on 1/1/62. Equipped with B-47 from 1/59 until 10/61.

307 BW(M) Equipped with B-47 at Lincoln AFB, Nebraska in 1955, retaining this type until discontinued and inactivated on 25/3/65.

370 BS(M) Utilized B-47 from 1955 until discontinued and inactivated on 25/3/65.

371 BS(M) Utilized B-47 from 1955 until discontinued and inactivated on 25/3/65.

372 BS(M) Utilized B-47 from 1955 until discontinued and inactivated on 25/3/65.

424 BS Redesignated from 424 BS(L) to 424 BS(M) on 11/8/58 and activated on 1/9/58 to support 307 BW alert commitment. Probably not operational from 10/61 until discontinued and inactivated on 1/1/62. Equipped with B-47 from 9/58 until 10/61.

4362 SS Organized at Lincoln AFB, Nebraska on 20/7/62 with EB-47L and attached to 307 BW but did not become operational until circa 31/7/62. Redesignated as 4362 PACCS during 1964, only to be inactivated on 24/12/64.

308 BW(M) Converted from B-29 to B-47 at Hunter AFB, Georgia in 1/54 and continued to operate this type until 15/7/59 when relocated to Plattsburgh AFB, New York where it was discontinued and inactivated on 25/6/61. Whilst at Plattsburgh, the 308 BW was not equipped, having a manning roster of just one officer and one airman, its aircraft being redistributed between the two 'super-strength' Wings.

373 BS(M) Utilized B-47 from 1/54 until 7/59. Not operational from 15/7/59 until discontinued and inactivated on 25/6/61.

374 BS(M) Utilized B-47 from 1/54 until 7/59. Not operational from 15/7/59 until discontinued and inactivated on 25/6/61.

375 BS(M) Utilized B-47 from 1/54 until 7/59. Not operational from 15/7/59 until discontinued and inactivated on 25/6/61.

425 BS Redesignated from 425 BS(H) to 425 BS(M) on 11/8/58 and activated on 1/10/58 to support 308 BW alert commitment. Not operational from 15/7/59 until discontinued and inactivated on 25/6/61. Equipped with B-47 from 10/58 until 7/59.

310 BW(M) Converted from B-29 to B-47 at Smoky Hill AFB, Kansas in 1954, retaining this type until 2/65. Redesignated 310 SAW on 1/3/62. Discontinued and inactivated 25/6/65.

379 BS(M) Utilized B-47 from 1954 until 2/65. Not operational from 25/2/65 until discontinued and inactivated on 25/3/65.

380 BS(M) Utilized B-47 from 1954 until 2/65. Not

operational from 25/2/65 until discontinued and inactivated on 25/3/65.

381 BS(M) Utilized B-47 from 1954 until 2/65. Not operational from 25/2/65 until discontinued and inactivated on 25/3/65.

428 BS(M) Activated on 1/2/59 to support 310 BW alert commitment. Not operational from 1/10/61 until discontinued and inactivated on 1/1/62. Equipped with B-47 from 2/59 until 10/61.

320 BW(M) Converted from B-29 to B-47 at March AFB, California in 7/53 and continued to operate this type until discontinued on 15/9/60.

441 BS(M) Utilized B-47 from 1953 to 5/60 and YRB-47 in 1953 only. Not operational from 16/5/60 until discontinued on 15/9/60.

442 BS(M) Utilized B-47 from 1953 until 8/60 and YRB-47 in 1953 only. Not operational from 1/9/60 until discontinued on 15/9/60.

443 BS(M) Utilized B-47 from 1953 until 8/60 and YRB-47 in 1953 only. Not operational from 1/9/60 until discontinued on 15/9/60.

444 BS Redesignated from 444 BS(L) to 444 BS(M) on 6/10/58 and activated on 1/1/59 to support 320 BW alert commitment. Not operational from 1/7/60 until discontinued on 15/9/60. Equipped with B-47 from 1/59 until 6/60.

321 BW(M) Established as 321 BW(M) on 23/3/53 and activated at Pinecastle AFB, Florida on 15/12/53 but not equipped with B-47 until 5/54. Retained B-47 until 9/61, being discontinued and inactivated on 25/10/61.

445 BS Redesignated from 445 BS(L) to 445 BS(M) on 25/11/53 and activated on 15/12/53. Utilized B-47 from 5/54 until 9/61. Not operational from circa 15/9/61 until discontinued and inactivated on 25/10/61. Was earmarked to operate DB-47/Bell Rascal pairing at one time.

446 BS Redesignated from 446 BS(L) to 446 BS(M) on 25/11/53 and activated on 15/12/53. Utilized B-47 from 5/54 until 9/61. Not operational from circa 15/9/61 until discontinued and inactivated on 25/10/61.

447 BS Redesignated from 447 BS(L) to 447 BS(M) on 25/11/53 and activated on 15/12/53. Utilized B-47 from 5/54 until 9/61. Not operational from circa 15/9/61 until discontinued and inactivated on 25/10/61.

448 BS Redesignated from 448 BS(L) to 448 BS(M) on 30/10/58 and activated on 1/2/59 to support 321 BW alert commitment. Not operational from 23/5/61 until discontinued and inactivated on 25/10/61. Equipped with B-47 from 2/59 until 5/61.

340 BW(M) Established as 340 BW(M) on 3/10/52 and activated at Sedalia AFB, Missouri on 20/10/52 but not equipped with B-47 until 4/54. Retained B-47 until mid-1963, subsequently being redesignated as 340 BW(H) on 1/9/63 and relocated to Bergstrom AFB, Texas to operate B-52Ds previously assigned to 4130 SW.

486 BS Redesignated from 486 BS(L) to 486 BS(M) on 3/10/52 and activated on 20/10/52. Utilized B-47 from 1954

until mid-1963 and YRB-47 during 1954–55. Redesignated 486 BS(H) on 1/9/63 to operate B-52D as part of 340 BW(H) at Bergstrom.

487 BS Redesignated from 487 BS(L) to 487 BS(M) on 3/10/52 and activated on 20/10/52. Utilized B-47 from 1954 until mid-1963 and YRB-47 during 1954–55. Discontinued and inactivated on 1/9/63.

488 BS Redesignated from 488 BS(L) to 488 BS(M) on 3/10/52 and activated on 20/10/52. Utilized B-47 from 1954 until mid-1963 and YRB-47 during 1954–55. Discontinued and inactivated on 1/9/63.

489 BS Redesignated from 489 BS(L) to 489 BS(M) on 11/8/58 and activated on 1/10/58 to support 340 BW alert commitment. Probably not operational between 10/61 and 1/1/62 when discontinued and inactivated. Equipped with B-47 from 10/58 until 10/61.

341 BW(M) Established as 341 BW(M) on 23/3/53 but not activated at Abilene AFB, Texas until 1/9/55. Equipped with B-47 from 1955 until discontinued and inactivated on 25/6/61.

10 BS Redesignated from 10 BS(L) to 10 BS(M) on 7/6/55 and activated on 1/9/55. Operated B-47 until discontinued and inactivated on 25/6/61.

12 BS Redesignated from 12 BS(L) to 12 BS(M) on 7/6/55 and activated on 1/9/55. Operated B-47 from 1956 until discontinued and inactivated on 25/6/61.

490 BS Redesignated from 490 BS(L) to 490 BS(M) on 7/6/55 and activated on 1/9/55. Operated B-47 from 1956 until discontinued and inactivated on 25/6/61.

491 BS Redesignated from 491 BS(L) to 491 BS(M) on 20/8/58 and activated on 1/11/58 to support 341 BW alert commitment. Operated B-47 from 11/58 until discontinued and inactivated on 25/6/61.

376 BW(M) Converted from B-29 to B-47 at Barksdale AFB, Louisiana in 2/54, retaining this type until discontinued and inactivated on 15/3/65. Relocated to Lockbourne AFB, Ohio on 1/12/57. Also used EB-47E and EB-47L at various times.

512 BS(M) Utilized B-47/EB-47E from 1954 until 15/3/65 when discontinued and inactivated.

513 BS(M) Utilized B-47/EB-47E from 1954 until 15/3/65 when discontinued and inactivated.

514 BS(M) Utilized B-47/EB-47E from 1954 until 15/3/65 when discontinued and inactivated.

515 BS Redesignated from 515 BS(H) to 515 BS(M) on 20/8/58 and activated on 1/12/58 to support 376 BW alert commitment. Not operational from circa 15/10/61 until discontinued and inactivated on 1/1/62. Equipped with B-47/EB-47E from 12/58 until 10/61.

4363 SS Organized at Lockbourne AFB, Ohio with EB-47L on 20/7/62 and attached to 376 BW but did not become operational until 11/62. Redesignated as 4363 PACCS during 1964 and remained with 376 BW until attached to 301 ARW on 15/3/65, subsequently being inactivated on 25/3/65.

379 BW(M) Established as 379 BW(M) on 23/3/53 but not activated at Homestead AFB, Florida until 1/11/55. Operated B-47 from 4/56 until late 1960, being redesignated as 379

BW(H) on 9/1/61 in anticipation of receiving B-52.

524 BS Redesignated from 524 BS(H) to 524 BS(M) on 12/7/55 and activated on 1/11/55. Utilized B-47 from 1956 until 1960. Redesignated 524 BS(H) on 9/1/61 and moved to Wurtsmith AFB, Mi., where it received B-52H, still as part of 379 BW.

525 BS Redesignated from 525 BS(H) to 525 BS(M) on 12/7/55 and activated on 1/11/55. Utilized B-47 from 1956 until 1960. Redesignated 525 BS(H) on 9/1/61 and reassigned to 19 BW at Homestead, in anticipation of receiving B-52H.

526 BS Redesignated from 526 BS(H) to 526 BS(M) on 12/7/55 and activated on 1/11/55. Utilized B-47 from 1956 until 1960. Redesignated 526 BS(H) on 9/1/61 and reassigned to 19 BW at Homestead, in anticipation of receiving B-52H.

527 BS Redesignated from 527 BS(H) to 527 BS(M) on 20/8/58 and activated 1/11/58 to support 379 BW alert commitment. Discontinued on 9/1/61. Equipped with B-47 from 11/58 until late 1960.

380 BW(M) Established as 380 BW(M) on 23/3/53 but not activated at Plattsburgh AFB, New York until 11/7/55. Utilized B-47 from 1955 until 12/65, being redesignated as the 380 SAW on 15/9/64. Received B-52G in 6/66. Was a 'superstrength' B-47 Wing.

528 BS(M) Activated on 11/7/55 and equipped with B-47 from 8/55 until 12/65. Redesignated 528 BS(H) circa 19/6/66 when received B-52G, having been non-operational since 14/12/65.

529 BS Redesignated from 529 BS(VH) to 529 BS(M) on 20/5/55 and activated on 11/7/55. Equipped with B-47 from 8/55 until 12/65. Not operational between 12/65 and 25/6/66 when discontinued and inactivated.

530 BS Redesignated from 530 BS(VH) to 530 BS(M) on 20/5/55 and activated on 11/7/55. Equipped with B-47 from 8/55 until 12/65. Not operational between 12/65 and 25/6/66 when discontinued and inactivated.

531 BS(M) Activated on 1/5/59 to support 380 BW alert commitment. Probably not operational from 10/61 until discontinued and inactivated on 1/1/62. Equipped with B-47 between 5/59 and 10/61.

4365 SS Organized at Plattsburgh AFB, New York with the EB-47L on 20/7/62 and attached to 380 BW. Redesignated 4365 PACCS during 1964 but was not operational between 12/9/64 and 24/12/64 when inactivated.

384 BW(M) Established as 384 BW(M) on 23/3/53 but not activated at Little Rock AFB, Arkansas until 1/8/55. Operated B-47 from 1956 until discontinued and inactivated on 1/9/64.

544 BS Redesignated from 544 BS(VH) to 544 BS(M) on 3/6/55 and activated on 1/8/55. Equipped with B-47 from 1956 until discontinued and inactivated on 1/9/64.

545 BS Redesignated from 545 BS(VH) to 545 BS(M) on 3/6/55 and activated on 1/8/55. Equipped with B-47 from 1956 until discontinued and inactivated on 1/9/64.

546 BS Redesignated from 546 BS(VH) to 546 BS(M) on 3/6/55 and activated on 1/8/55. Equipped with B-47 from 1956 until discontinued and inactivated on 1/9/64.

547 BS Redesignated from 547 BS(VH) to 547 BS(M) on 11/8/58 and activated on 1/9/58 to support 384 BW alert commitment. Probably not operational from 10/61 until discontinued and inactivated on 1/1/62. Equipped with B-47 from 9/58 until 10/61.

509 BW(M) Converted from B-50 to B-47 at Walker AFB, New Mexico in 6/55 and continued to operate B-47 until 11/65, moving to Pease AFB, New Hampshire on 1/7/58. Received B-52D in 3/66 and redesignated 509 BW(H) on 2/4/66.

393 BS(M) Utilized B-47 from 1955 until 11/65. Not operational from 23/11/65 until 22/3/66 when received B-52D, being subsequently redesignated as 393 BS(H).

661 BS(M) Activated 1/3/59 to support 509 BW alert commitment. Not operational from 15/10/61 until 1/1/62 when inactivated. Equipped with the B-47 from 3/59 until 10/61.

715 BS(M) Utilized B-47 from 1955 until 11/65. Not operational from 23/11/65 until 25/6/66 when inactivated.

830 BS(M) Utilized B-47 from 1955 until 11/65. Not operational from 23/11/65 until 25/6/66 when inactivated.

4347 CCTW Formerly 3520 FTW with Air Training Command at McConnell AFB, Kansas, being transferred to SAC as 4347 CCTW on 1/7/58. Inactivated 15/6/63. Used B/TB-47 from 7/58 until 6/63.

4347/4348/4349/4350 CCTS.

Index